JANICE VANCLEAVE'S

# Guide to the
# Best Science Fair
# Projects

Janice VanCleave

SCHOLASTIC INC.

New York   Toronto   London   Auckland   Sydney
Mexico City   New Delhi   Hong Kong

This book is dedicated to a very knowledgeable and talented teacher, whose help in writing this book was invaluable. What a pleasure it has been to work with my friend and colleague, Holly Ruiz.

## Acknowledgments

I would like to thank Laura Roberts Fields and Ann Skrabanek for their support and helpful ideas. A special note of thanks to John Cook, my production editor, for his patience and time needed for this project.

ISBN 0-439-07059-7

# CONTENTS

# I

# A GUIDE TO
# SCIENCE FAIR
# PROJECTS

# Chapter 1

# How to Use This Book

So you're going to do a science fair project. Great! Your work could be chosen as an entry in your school fair and even in regional, state, or national competitions. As a participant in any science fair, you'll get to show off your work and possibly receive achievement awards. But most important, you'll also learn a lot about science by observing and sharing with other fair participants.

A **science project** is like a mystery in which you are the detective searching for answers. Science projects let you practice and exhibit your detective skills. You not only get to select which mystery to solve, but you can creatively design methods for uncovering clues that will lead to the final revelation of who, what, when, where, how, and why. This book will give you guidance and ideas. It's your job to discover the answers!

Solving a scientific mystery, like solving a detective mystery, requires planning and the careful collection of facts. Trying to assemble a project overnight may result in frustration and cheats you out of the fun of being a science detective. With a little planning, though, your science fair experience can be positive and rewarding. This book shows you how to plan ahead. It also gives you the skills and techniques to turn simple experiments into competitive science fair projects. So before you start experimenting, read all of Part I. It explains the eight most important points you need to know for science fair success. These eight points are:

1. *The scientific method.* Thinking about solutions to problems and testing each possibility for the best solution is what the scientific method is all about. Chapter 2 describes the steps of the scientific method and how all scientists use this basic tool.

2. *Topic research.* Selecting a topic is often considered the hardest part of a science fair project. The research suggestions in Chapter 3 will help make choosing a topic enjoyable. **Research** is the process of collecting information and data. **Data** as used in this book is observations and/or measured facts obtained experimentally. **Topic research** is research used to select a project topic.

3. *Categories.* Chapter 4 provides a list of categories that are used in science fairs. You should identify the category that your project falls into at the beginning of your research. Judges base their evaluation of the content of your project on the category in which you enter it. For example, an A+ botany project incorrectly entered in the math category most likely will receive a lower rating.

4. *Project research.* Once you have selected a topic, it's time to find out as much about it as possible. **Project research** helps you understand a topic. This involves more than just reading materials you find in the library; you'll want to interview people who know a lot about the topic and do exploratory experiments. **Exploratory experiments** as defined in this book are experiments used to gather research. Chapter 5 provides suggestions and directions for doing these. This chapter also gives instructions for requesting printed

information from people and organizations.

5. *A sample project.* Chapter 6 guides you step-by-step through the collection of research and its use in identifying a **problem** (a scientific question to be solved), proposing a hypothesis, and designing a project experiment. A **hypothesis** is an idea about the solution to a problem, based on knowledge and research. A **project experiment** is an experiment designed to test a hypothesis. The instructions in this chapter will be invaluable to you as you prepare your own project.

6. *The project report.* A **project report** is the written record of your entire project from start to finish. Chapter 7 shows you how to write a project report after you have completed your project. Your teacher will tell you the level of detail to use in your report. This book gives instructions that can be used for a simple or a complex report.

7. *The display.* Displaying the project can be a fun experience. The examples in Chapter 8 for constructing a backboard should make the experience easy and enjoyable.

8. *Presentation and evaluation.* Chapter 9 helps to prepare you to be judged and tells you what to expect at the fair.

Part II provides project research and ideas for planning and developing projects on 50 science fair topics. These are not intended to be complete projects themselves, but to offer guidelines in developing your own project. The fun of a science fair project lies in exploring a topic in which you're interested, finding and recording information, planning the project experiment, organizing the data, and reaching a conclusion. A science fair project allows you to make your own discoveries. If you have an enthusiastic attitude, you can do it! Let's get started!

# Chapter 2

# The Scientific Method

A science project is an investigation using the scientific method to discover the answer to a scientific problem. Before starting your project, you need to understand the scientific method. This chapter uses examples to illustrate and explain the basic steps of the scientific method. Chapters 3 through 5 give more details, and Chapter 6 uses the scientific method in a sample project. The **scientific method** is the "tool" that scientists use to find the answers to questions. It is the process of thinking through the possible solutions to a problem and testing each possibility for the best solution. The scientific method involves the following steps: doing research, identifying the problem, stating a hypothesis, conducting project experimentation, and reaching a conclusion.

## RESEARCH

Research is the process of collecting information from your own experiences, knowledgeable sources, and data from exploratory experiments. Your first research is used to select a project topic. This is called topic research. For example, you observe different seeds in the kitchen and wonder if they will grow. Because of this experience, you decide to learn how seeds grow. Your topic will be about **germination.**

Once the topic is selected, you begin what is called project research. This is research to help you understand the topic, express a problem, propose a hypothesis, and design one or more project experiments—experiments designed to test the hypothesis. An example of project research would be planting pinto beans as an exploratory experiment. The result of

this experiment and other research gives you the needed information for the next step—identifying the problem.

> **Do** use many references from printed sources—books, journals, magazines, and newspapers—as well as electronic sources—computer software and on-line services.
>
> **Do** gather information from professionals—instructors, librarians, and scientists, such as physicians and veterinarians.
>
> **Do** perform other exploratory experiments such as those in the 50 science project ideas in Part II.

## PROBLEM

The problem is the scientific question to be solved. It is best expressed as an "open-ended" question, which is a question that is answered with a statement, not just a yes or no. For example, "How does light affect the germination of bean seeds?"

> **Do** limit your problem. Note that the previous question is about one period of seed development and one type of seed instead of all seeds. To find the answer to a question such as "How does light affect seeds?" would require that you test different periods of seed development and an extensive variety of seed types.
>
> **Do** choose a problem that can be solved experimentally. For example, the question "What is a flashlight?" can be answered by finding the definition of the word *flashlight* in the dictionary. "What makes a flashlight bulb glow?" can be answered by experimentation.

## HYPOTHESIS

A hypothesis is an idea about the solution to a problem, based on knowledge and research. While the hypothesis is a single statement, it is the key to a successful project. All of your project research is done with the goal of expressing a problem, proposing an answer to it—the hypothesis, and designing project experimentation. Then, all of your project experimenting will be performed to test the hypothesis. The hypothesis should make a claim about how two factors relate. For example, in the following sample hypothesis, the two relating factors are light and seed germination. One example of a hypothesis for the earlier problem question is:

"I believe that bean seeds do not need light during germination. I base my hypothesis on these facts:

• Seed packages instruct the user to plant seeds beneath the soil where it is dark.

• In my exploratory experiment, pinto beans germinated beneath the surface of soil in the absence of light."

**Do** state facts from past experiences or observations on which you based your hypothesis.

**Do** write down your hypothesis before beginning the project experimentation.

**Don't** change your hypothesis even if experimentation does not support it. If time permits, repeat or redesign the experiment.

## PROJECT EXPERIMENTATION

Project experimentation is the process of testing a hypothesis. The things that have an effect on the experiment are called **variables**. There are three kinds of variables that you need to identify in your experiments: independent, dependent, and controlled. The **independent variable** is the variable you purposely manipulate (change). The **dependent variable** is the variable being observed that changes in response to the independent variable. The variables that are not changed are called **controlled variables.**

The problem in this chapter concerns the effect of light on seed germination. The independent variable for the experiment is light and the dependent variable is seed germination. Other factors could cause the dependent variable to change. To be sure that they don't affect the outcome, a **control** is set up. In a control, all variables are identical to the experimental setup—your original setup—except for the independent variable. Factors that are identical in both the experimental setup and the control setup are the controlled variables. For example, prepare the experiment by planting 3 or 4 different beans, one bean type per container. Place the containers in a dark closet so that they receive no light. If at the end of a set time period, the seeds grow, you might decide that no light was needed for germination. But, before making this decision, you must determine experimentally if the seeds would grow with light. Thus, a control group of plants must be set up so that the container receives light throughout the testing period. The other variables for the experimental and control setup, such as type of container, soil, amount of water, temperature, and type of seeds used must be kept the same. These are controlled variables.

**Do** have only one independent variable during an experiment.

**Do** repeat the experiment more than once to verify your results if time permits.

**Do** organize data. (See Chapter 6, "A Sample Project," for information on organizing data from experiments.)

**Do** have a control.

## PROJECT CONCLUSION

The project conclusion is a summary of the results of the project experimentation and a statement of how the results relate to the hypothesis. Reasons for experimental results that are contrary to the hypothesis are included. If applicable, the conclusion can end by giving ideas for further testing.

*If your results do not support your hypothesis:*

**Don't** change your hypothesis.

**Don't** leave out experimental results that do not support your hypothesis.

**Do** give possible reasons for the difference between your hypothesis and the experimental results.

**Do** give ways that you can experiment further to find a solution.

*If your results support your hypothesis:*

For example, you might say, "As stated in my hypothesis, I believe that light is not necessary during the germination of bean seeds. My experimentation supports the idea that bean seeds will germinate without light. After 7 days, the seeds tested were seen growing in full light and no light. It is possible that some light reached the "no light" containers that were placed in a dark closet. If I were to improve on this experiment, I would place the "no light" containers in a light-proof box and/or wrap them in a light-proof material, such as aluminum foil."

# Chapter 3

# Topic Research

Now that you understand the scientific method, you are ready to get started.

## KEEP A JOURNAL

Purchase a bound notebook to serve as your **journal.** This notebook should contain topic and project research. It should contain not only your original ideas but also ideas you get from printed sources or from people. It should also include descriptions of your exploratory and project experiments as well as diagrams, graphs, and written observations of all your results.

Every entry should be as neat as possible and dated. A neat, orderly journal provides a complete and accurate record of your project from start to finish, and it can be used to write your project report. It is also proof of the time you spent searching out the answers to the scientific mystery you undertook to solve. You will want to display the journal with your completed project.

## SELECTING A TOPIC

Obviously you want to get an A+ on your project, win awards at the science fair, and learn many new things about science. Some or all of these goals are possible, but you will have to spend a lot of time working on your project, so choose a topic that interests you. It is best to pick a topic and stick with it, but if you find after some work that your topic is not as interesting as you originally thought, stop and select another one. Since it takes time to develop a good project, it is unwise to repeatedly jump from one topic to another. You may in fact decide to stick with your original idea even if it is not as exciting as you had expected. You might just uncover some very interesting facts that you didn't know.

Remember that the objective of a science project is to learn more about science. Your project doesn't have to be highly complex to be successful. Excellent projects can be developed that answer very basic and fundamental questions about events or situations encountered on a daily basis. There are many easy ways of selecting a topic. The following are just a few of them.

## LOOK CLOSELY AT THE WORLD AROUND YOU

You can turn everyday experiences into a project topic by using the "exploring" question "I wonder…?" For example, you often see cut flowers in a vase of water. These flowers stay pretty for days. If you express this as an exploring question—"I wonder, why do cut flowers last so long in a vase of water?"—you have a good question about plants. But could this be a project topic? Think about it! Is it only the water in the vase that keeps the flowers fresh? Does it matter how the flower stems are cut? By continuing to ask questions, you zero in on the topic of water movement through plants.

Keep your eyes and ears open, and start asking yourself more exploring questions, such as "I wonder, why does my dad paint our house so often?" "I wonder, do different brands of paint last longer?" "I wonder, could I test different kinds of paint on small pieces of wood?" To know more about these things, you can research and design a whole science fair project about the topic of the durability of different kinds of paint. You will be pleasantly surprised at the number of possible project ideas that will come to mind when you begin to look around and use "exploring" questions.

There are an amazing number of comments stated and questions asked by you and those around you each day that could be used to develop science project topics. Be alert and listen for a statement such as "He's a chip off the old block, a southpaw like his dad." If you are in the searching phase of your science fair project, this statement can become an exploring question, such as, "I wonder, what percentage of people are left-handed?" or "I wonder, are there more left-handed boys than girls?" These questions could lead you to developing a project about the topic of genetics (inheriting characteristics from one's parents).

## CHOOSE A TOPIC FROM YOUR EXPERIENCE

Having a cold is not pleasant, but you could use this "distasteful" experience as a means of selecting a project topic. For example, you may remember that when you had a cold, food did not taste as good. Ask yourself, "I wonder, was this because my nose was stopped up and I couldn't smell the food?" A project about taste and smell could be very successful. After research, you might decide on a problem question such as "How does smell affect taste?" Propose your hypothesis and start designing your project experiment. For more on developing a project, see Chapter 6, "A Sample Project."

## FIND A TOPIC IN SCIENCE MAGAZINES

Don't expect topic ideas in science magazines to include detailed instructions on how to perform experiments and design displays. What you can look for are facts that interest you and that lead you to ask exploring questions. An article about Antarctic animals might bring to mind these exploring questions: "I wonder, how do penguins stay warm?" "I wonder, do fat penguins stay warmer than skinny penguins?" Wow! Body insulation, another great project topic.

## SELECT A TOPIC FROM A BOOK ON SCIENCE FAIR PROJECTS OR SCIENCE EXPERIMENTS

Science fair project books, such as this one, can provide you with many different topics to choose from. Even though science experiment books do not give you as much direction as science fair project books, many can provide you with exploratory "cookbook" experiments that tell you what to do, what the results should be, and why. But it will be up to you to provide all the exploring questions and ideas for further experimentation. The 50 project ideas described in this book can further sharpen your skills at expressing exploring questions. A list of different project and experiment books can be found in Appendix A.

## SOMETHING TO CONSIDER

You are encouraged not to experiment with vertebrate animals or bacteria. If you do wish to include them in your project, ask your teacher about special permission forms required by your local fair organization. Supervision by a professional, such as a veterinarian or physician, is usually required. The project must cause no harm or undue stress to the subject.

# Chapter 4

# Categories

Every fair has a list of categories, and you need to seek your teacher's advice when deciding which category you should enter your project in. It is important that you enter your project in the correct category. Since science fair judges are required to judge the content of each project based on the category in which it is entered, you would be seriously penalized if you were to enter your project in the wrong category. Listed here are common science fair categories with a brief description of each. Some topics can correctly be placed in more than one category; for example, the structure of plants could be in botany or anatomy. Each of the 50 project ideas in Part II is labeled with the category in which the project could be entered. The categories are:

- **astronomy:** The study of stars, planets, and other objects in the universe.

- **biology:** The study of living things.

  1. **anatomy:** The study of the structure of plants and animals.

  2. **behaviorism:** The study of actions that alter the relationship between an organism, such as a plant or an animal, and its environment.

  3. **botany:** The study of plants and plant life, including their structure and growth.

  4. **ecology:** The study of the relationships of living things to other living things and to their environment.

  5. **genetics:** The study of the methods of transmission of qualities from parents to their offspring; the principles of heredity in living things.

  6. **microbiology:** The study of microscopic organisms, such as, fungi, bacteria, and protista.

  7. **physiology:** The study of life processes, such as respiration, circulation, the nervous system, metabolism, and reproduction.

  8. **zoology:** The study of animals, including their structure and growth.

- **earth science:** The study of the earth.

  1. **geology:** The study of the earth, including the composition of its layers, its crust, and its history. Subtopics may include the following:

     a. **fossils:** Remnants or traces of prehistoric life-forms preserved in the earth's crust.

     b. **mineralogy:** The study of the composition and formation of minerals.

     c. **rocks:** Solids made up of one or more minerals.

     d. **seismology:** The study of earthquakes.

     e. **volcanology:** The study of volcanoes.

  2. **meteorology:** The study of weather, climate, and the earth's atmosphere.

  3. **oceanography:** The study of the oceans and marine organisms.

**4. paleontology:** The study of prehistoric life-forms.

- **engineering:** The application of scientific knowledge for practical purposes.

- **physical science:** The study of matter and energy.

  **1. chemistry:** The study of the materials that substances are made of and how they change and combine.

  **2. physics:** The study of forms of energy and the laws of motion. Subtopics include studies in the following areas:

    **a. electricity:** The form of energy associated with the presence and movement of electric charges.

    **b. energy:** The capacity to do work.

    **c. gravity:** The force that pulls celestial bodies, such as planets and moons, toward each other; the force that pulls things on or near a celestial body toward its center.

    **d. machines:** Devices that make work easier.

    **e. magnetism:** The force of attraction or repulsion between magnetic poles, and the attraction that magnets have for magnetic materials.

- **mathematics:** The use of numbers and symbols to study amounts and forms.

  **1. geometry:** The branch of mathematics that deals with points, lines, planes, and their relationships to each other.

# Chapter 5

# Project Research

Once you have completed the topic research and selected a topic, you are ready to begin your project research. This research is generally more thorough than topic research. Project research is the process of collecting information from knowledgeable sources, such as books, magazines, software, librarians, teachers, parents, scientists, or other professionals. It is also data collected from exploratory experimentation. Read widely on the topic you selected so that you understand it and know about the findings of others. Be sure to give credit where credit is due and record all information and data in your journal.

How successful you are with your project will depend largely on how well you understand your topic. The more you read and question people who know something about your topic, the broader your understanding will be. As a result, it will be easier for you to explain your project to other people, especially a science fair judge. There are two basic kinds of research—primary and secondary.

## PRIMARY RESEARCH

**Primary research** is information you collect on your own. This includes information from exploratory experiments you perform, surveys you take, interviews, and responses to your letters.

Interview people who have special knowledge about your topic. These can include teachers, doctors, scientists, or others whose careers require them to know something related to your topic. Let's say your topic is

about the speed of dinosaurs. "Who would know about dinosaurs?" Start with your science teacher. He or she may have a special interest in dinosaurs or know someone who does. Is there a museum with dinosaur exhibits nearby? Owners of rock and mineral shops may have an interest in fossils and could provide information. Contact the geology department of a local university.

Before contacting the person(s) you want to interview, be prepared. You can do this by making a list of questions that you want to ask. You can even discuss what you know about your topic with someone who knows nothing about it. In so doing, you will be forced to organize your thinking and may even discover additional questions to add to your list. Once your list is complete, you are ready to make your call. Simple rules of courtesy, such as the following, will better ensure that the person called is willing to help.

1. Identify yourself.

2. Identify the school you attend and your teacher.

3. Briefly explain why you are calling. Include information about your project and explain how the person can help you.

4. Request an interview time that is convenient for the person. This could be a telephone or face-to-face interview. Be sure to say that the interview will take about 20 to 30 minutes.

5. Ask if you may tape-record the interview. You can get more information if you are not trying to write down all the answers. It

may be that the person is free when you call, so be prepared to start the interview.

6. Be on time, and be ready to start the interview immediately. Also, be courteous and end the interview on time.

7. Thank the person for the time given and the information provided.

8. A written thank-you note should be sent after the interview, so be sure to record the person's name and address.

You may write letters requesting information instead of interviewing, or write letters in addition to interviewing. Check at the end of articles in periodicals for lists of names and addresses where more information can be obtained. Your librarian can assist you in locating current periodicals related to your topic. If your project deals with a household product, check the packaging for the address of the manufacturer. Send your letter to the public relations department. Ask for all available printed material about your topic. Send your letter as soon as possible to allow time for material to be sent. You can use a form letter similar to the one shown here to make it easier to send it to as many different people and organizations as you can find.

---

Lacey Russell
231 Kids Lane
Woodlands, OK 74443

August 31, 2005

The Dial Corporation
15101 North Scottsdale Road
Station 5028
Scottsdale, AZ 85254

Dear Director:

I am a sixth-grade student currently working on a science project for the Davin Elementary Science Fair. My project is about conditions affecting bacterial growth. I would greatly appreciate any information you could send me on the "anti-bacterial" properties of your product. Please send the information as soon as possible.

Thank you very much.

Sincerely,


Lacey Russell

---

## SECONDARY RESEARCH

**Secondary research** is information and/or data that someone else has collected. You find this type of information in written sources (books, magazines, and newspapers) and in electronic sources (CD-ROM encyclopedias, software packages, or on-line services, such as the Internet). When you use a secondary source, be sure to note where you got the information for future reference. If you are required to write a report, you will need the following information for a bibliography or to give credit for any quotes or illustrations you use.

*Book*

Author's name, title of book, place of publication, publisher, copyright date, and pages read or quoted.

*Magazine or periodical*

Author's name, title of article, title of magazine, volume number and date of publication, and page numbers of article.

*Newspaper*

Author's name, title of article, name of newspaper, date of publication, and section and page numbers.

*Encyclopedia*

Title of article, name of encyclopedia, volume number, place of publication, publisher, year of publication, and page numbers of article.

*CD-ROM encyclopedia or software package*

Name of program, version or release number, name of supplier, and place where supplier is located.

*Documents from on-line services*

Author of document (if known), title of document, name of organization that posted document, place where organization is located, date given on document, on-line address or mailing address where document is available.

## USE YOUR RESEARCH

Now you are ready to use the project research information and data collected to express the problem, propose a hypothesis, and design and perform one or more project experiments. The project research will also be useful in writing the project report. The following chapters, 6 through 9, guide you step-by-step through a sample project from start to finish. You may want to read these chapters more than once and refer back to them as you progress through your project.

# Chapter 6

# A Sample Project

Pick a topic. Each of the 50 project ideas in Part II begins with a detailed exploratory experiment. Read some or all of these easy experiments to discover the topic you like best and want to know more about. Regardless of the topic you choose for the science fair, what you discover from any of these experiments will make you more knowledgeable about science.

How can you turn a project idea from this book into your own unique project?

This chapter uses a project idea similar in format to those found in Part II. The detailed exploratory experiment will be referred to as the sample experiment, and is used for several purposes. Like all exploratory experiments, its main purpose is to provide research data on which to base a hypothesis. But in this chapter, it is also used as a model for a project experiment. During the experimentation phase of your project, you can use the following data-collecting techniques and other ideas to design, develop, and fine-tune your project.

## KEEPING YOUR PROJECT JOURNAL

Every step of the way, you will keep a journal in which to record the progress of the project. After experimentation has been completed, the journal will be very useful to you when you begin to write your project report. Chapter 7 explains how to write a project report.

## TITLE AND PROBLEM QUESTION

The title and problem question for the sample experiment (see Figure 6.1) may or may

---

# More Heat

### PROBLEM

*Which warms faster, water or soil?*

**Figure 6.1  Sample Experiment Title and Problem**

---

### Materials

knife (to be used only by an adult)
small box at least 10 inches (25 cm)
 square
two 9-ounce (270-ml) paper cups
light-colored soil
tap water
2 thermometers
ruler
duct tape
paper
pencil
timer
desk lamp
adult helper

**Figure 6.2  Sample Experiment Materials List**

---

not be acceptable for your project. Because you'll know so much more after doing the sample experiment and other research, let's wait before deciding on the title and problem question.

## MATERIALS

As Figure 6.2 shows, all the materials for the sample experiment, like those for all the experiments in this book, can be found around the house or purchased without much money at a local grocery or hardware store. Collect the supplies before you start the experiment. You will have less frustration and more fun if all the materials are ready before you start.

Substituting materials is not suggested, but if something is not available, ask an adult's advice before using different materials.

Note that each of the project ideas in Part II contains more than one exploratory experiment. The "Materials" section at the beginning of each project contains only the materials for the first experiment. Be sure to read through the entire project prior to starting to determine all the materials you'll need to complete each experiment.

## PROCEDURE

The "Procedure" section for the sample experiment contains the steps needed to complete the experiment. As described in Chapter 2, a variable is anything that has an effect on the experiment. In the sample experiment, water and soil are tested to see which surface warms faster. The type of surface being tested is the independent, or manipulated, variable. Each surface absorbs a certain amount of heat from the lamp. The resulting change in temperature of each surface is the dependent, or responding, variable. All other variables, such as the amount of light that the surfaces receive, the amount of water and soil tested, the containers for the test materials, and, generally, the total environment around each container (room temperature, humidity, etc.), are the controlled, or constant, variables. Note: Approximate metric equivalents have been given after all English measurements.

Remember, this sample experiment is part of your project research. Have someone take

**Procedure**

1. Ask an adult to cut off the top and one side of the box.

2. Fill one cup with soil and the other with water.

3. Place the cups together at the back of the box.

4. Put a thermometer in each cup. The bulb of each thermometer should be about ¼ inch (0.63 cm) below the surface of the water or soil in the cup.

5. Tape the top of each thermometer to the back of the box.

6. Prepare a chart to record the experimental results.

7. After the thermometers have been in the cups for at least 5 minutes, record the temperature of each material. These are the starting temperatures.

8. Place the box under the lamp so that the lightbulb is about 10 inches (25 cm) from the top of the cups and centered over them. Make sure that the lightbulb does not touch the box.

9. After 10 minutes, turn the lamp off and immediately record the temperature in each cup. These are the final temperatures.

10. Calculate and record the changes between the starting temperatures and the final temperatures.

*Figure 6.3   Sample Experiment Procedure*

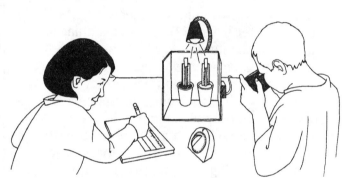

*Figure 6.4   Procedure Setup*

a photograph of you performing the experiment, as in Figure 6.4, or take photos of the procedure setup to use as part of the project display. Use the format of the procedure shown in Figure 6.3 as a guideline to design your own project experiment.

### TEMPERATURE CHANGES FOR SOIL AND WATER

| Material | Temperature (°F) | | |
| --- | --- | --- | --- |
| | Starting | Final | Change |
| light-colored soil | 75 | 82 | 7 |
| tap water | 73 | 77 | 4 |

*Figure 6.5   Table and Bar Graph for Sample Experiment*

**TEMPERATURE CHANGES FOR SOIL AND WATER**

Temperature (°F) Change

light-colored soil

water

Material

| SOIL SURFACE TEMPERATURE (Direct Light) | |
|---|---|
| Time (min.) | Temperature (°F) |
| 0 | 77 |
| 5 | 83 |
| 10 | 82 |
| 15 | 84 |
| 20 | 84 |
| 25 | 85 |
| 30 | 86 |

***Figure 6.6   Example of a Table***

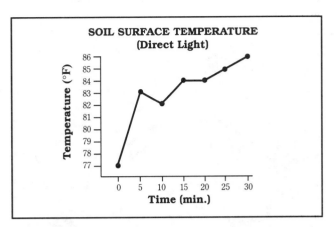

***Figure 6.8   Example of a Line Graph***

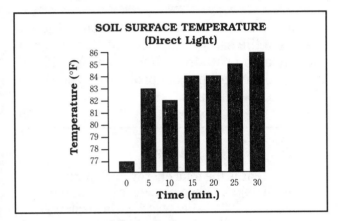

***Figure 6.7   Example of a Bar Graph***

## RESULTS

Before you can state the results of an experiment, you must first organize all the data collected during experimentation. Numbers, called "raw data," have little meaning unless you organize and label them. Data from each experiment needs to be written down in an orderly way in your journal. Use a **table** (a diagram that uses words and numbers in columns and rows to represent data) to record data. Use a graph, such as a **bar graph** (a diagram that uses bars to represent data) similar to the one shown in Figure 6.5 to **analyze** (separate and examine) data.

Figures 6.6 through 6.8 give examples of three different ways to express the same data for surface temperature of soil. Figure 6.6 shows another example of a table, Figure 6.7 shows a bar graph, and Figure 6.8 shows a **line graph** (a diagram that uses lines to express patterns of change).

There are other useful ways to represent data. A circle graph, or **pie chart**, is a **chart** (data or other information in the form of a table, graph, or list) that shows information in percentages. The larger the section of the circle, the greater the percentage represented. The whole circle represents 100 percent, or the total amount. For example, a pie chart can be used to represent the results of an experiment measuring soil surface temperatures for June. To make a pie chart, first record the number and percentage of days that have each average daily temperature in a table, as shown in Figure 6.9. Then, express the same data as percentages in a pie chart, as shown in Figure 6.10. Note that illustrations of children are placed around the circle to add interest to the data display.

| SOIL SURFACE TEMPERATURES FOR JUNE | | |
|---|---|---|
| Average Daily Temperature (°F) | Number of Days | Percentage of Days |
| 90 | 12 | 40% |
| 91 | 9 | 30% |
| 92 | 6 | 20% |
| 93 | 3 | 10% |

***Figure 6.9   Table of Soil Surface Temperatures***

*Figure 6.10   Pie Chart of Soil Surface Temperatures*

A pictograph could be used to represent the results of an experiment measuring wind speeds. A **pictograph** is a chart that contains symbols representing data, such as quantities of an object. In the pictograph shown in Figure 6.11, each flag represents wind speed of 1 mile per hour. Pictographs are easy to read and can add a little fun to your data display.

The data charted in Figure 6.5 was used to write a statement of the changes in temperature of the soil and water in the sample project, as shown in Figure 6.12.

## WHY?

Figure 6.13 shows an explanation of the results of the sample experiment. This information, along with the other research, will be used to develop a project problem, hypothesis, and experiment(s).

### WIND SPEED (6/1–6/3)

| Date | | Each ⊐ = 1 mph |
|------|------|------|
| 6/1 | Day | ⊐ ⊐ ⊐ ⊐ |
| | Night | ⊐ ⊐ ⊐ |
| 6/2 | Day | ⊐ ⊐ ⊐ ⊐ ⊐ |
| | Night | ⊐ ⊐ ⊐ ⊐ |
| 6/3 | Day | ⊐ ⊐ ⊐ ⊐ |
| | Night | ⊐ ⊐ ⊐ ⊐ |

*Figure 6.11   Example of a Pictograph*

### Results

After 10 minutes under the lamp, the temperature of the soil changed 7 degrees and the temperature of the water changed 4 degrees.

*Figure 6.12   Sample Experiment Results*

### Why?

**Heat** is the total energy of all particles in an object. When heat energy from the light is added to the object, its total energy increases. While the addition of heat usually causes the temperature of the object to increase, the same amount of heat does not cause the same change in temperature in all substances. The amount of heat needed to raise the temperature of 1 pound of a substance 1 degree Fahrenheit (1 g of a substance 1°C) is called **specific heat.**

Although the same amount of heat is added to both cups, the temperature change is not the same for the two materials. Water does not heat up as quickly as soil does; thus, water has a higher specific heat than the soil.

*Figure 6.13   Sample Experiment "Why?"*

## LET'S EXPLORE

This is the point at which you begin to ask different exploring questions as the basis for more research ideas, such as "I wonder, does soil cool faster than water?" or "I wonder, does the color of soil affect the rate at which its temperature changes? Wow! That last question is great." You'll find that the more you think about the sample experiment, the more exploring questions you'll be able to think of and the better your questions will be. Figure 6.14 shows exploring questions and how to find their answers by changing the sample experiment. The experiments in this and the following sections could be performed and the data added to the research information. Another use would be as aids in designing your project experiment(s). Before any further experimentation, read through "Let's Explore," "Show Time!", and "Check It Out!"

---

### LET'S EXPLORE

1. Do the materials cool at the same rate? Repeat the experiment, but record the temperatures as soon as the lamp has been turned off as the starting temperature. After the lamp has been off for 10 minutes, record the temperatures as the final temperatures. Calculate the temperature change for each cup.

2. Does the color of the soil affect the amount of heat needed to change its temperature? Repeat the original experiment, using soils of different colors. You may want to collect soil samples from different locations during a vacation or ask friends to send you soil. Use red, black, and other colors of soil.

---

*Figure 6.14   Sample Experiment "Let's Explore"*

## SHOW TIME!

The "Show Time!" section in Figure 6.15 shows two ideas related to the sample experiment. It offers different experimental ideas for further investigation of the topic, as well as more ideas for designing your own

experiments. (When you design your own experiments, make sure to get an adult's approval if you use supplies or procedures other than those given in this book.) Again, these experiments can provide project research or ideas for designing your project experiment(s).

---

### SHOW TIME!

1. Is the temperature of the air above the materials affected when the materials are heated? Fill two 9-ounce (270-ml) paper cups half full, one with water and the other with dark-colored soil. Place the cups in the open box. Hold a thermometer in each cup so that the bulb is just above the surface of the material, and secure it to the box with tape. After 5 minutes, record the temperature of the air. Remove the thermometers and heat the cups under a lamp for 10 minutes as in the original experiment. Place a thermometer in each cup as before, then record the air temperature above the heated materials.

2. Do structures affect the earth's surface temperature? Read and record the temperatures on 2 thermometers. Place one thermometer on the ground (on either grass or soil) in the shade of a tree, building, or other large structure. Place the second thermometer on the same type of surface, but in direct sunlight. Record the temperatures on both thermometers every 5 minutes for 30 minutes. Use graphs to display the results.

---

*Figure 6.15   Sample Experiment "Show Time!"*

## CHECK IT OUT!

At this point, you are ready for in-depth research on the topic. The questions asked at this point (see Figure 6.16) require some secondary research. A good place to start your research is the library. Earth science books have sections on weather, air temperature, and wind production. Science experiment books are also a good source of information and provide experiments to use as well.

You will discover from these sources that warm air rises and cold air sinks, and that wind moves from cool areas toward warmer areas. Wow! That's just like at the beach when the breezes blow in toward the land during the day and out to sea at night. This is a real-life experience that you are using to help you with your project. You will want to draw from your personal experiences, not only when looking for a topic as discussed in Chapter 3, but during your project research.

---

### CHECK IT OUT!

The difference in the specific heat of the earth's land and water surfaces causes differences in their surface temperatures. Find out how different surface temperatures affect weather. How does surface temperature affect air temperature? What effect does air temperature have on wind production?

---

*Figure 6.16  Sample Experiment "Check It Out!"*

## PROBLEM AND HYPOTHESIS

After collecting and analyzing your project research, it's time to zero in on the problem. Let's say you've decided to investigate the effect of surface temperature on wind direction. The question doesn't have to be complex and wordy to be good. Make it as simple and to the point as possible. Look at these two examples:

**1.** How does the change in temperature of sand and water affect wind direction at the beach?

**2.** Does the difference in the change in temperature of sand and water cause the air above these surfaces to move at different rates? If so, how does that difference affect the production of sea and land breezes?

Both of the examples have the same goal of discovering how sea and land breezes are produced, but the first example is short and quickly read. Keep in mind that your project will be judged at the science fair, and you want each judge to know immediately the single purpose for your project.

With your problem stated, it's time to developed the hypothesis. The hypothesis might be "I believe that there is a difference in the rate of change in the temperature of sand and water, resulting in a change of wind direction at the beach." This hypothesis is based on these facts:

- In my exploratory experiment, water heated more slowly than the soil during the same period of time.

- Water and land surfaces have different specific heats, thus it takes a greater gain or loss of heat to change the temperature of water than land surfaces.

- Winds move from cold areas to warm areas.

## NOW YOU'RE ON YOUR OWN

Test your hypothesis by replacing the soil with sand in the exploratory experiments. Design new experiments that test rate changes in the temperatures of the surfaces and the air above them. But an experiment relating surface temperature to wind direction will also be needed. Think! What moves in the wind? Flags and smoke do. You might test air motion by using lightweight materials or, with adult assistance, smoke. Once one or more experiments have been designed, collect data, construct tables and graphs, draw diagrams, and/or take photos to represent results.

## UNEXPECTED RESULTS?

What do you do if your results are not what you expected? First, if there is time, repeat the experiment and make sure everything is done properly. If there isn't time for this, or if you get the same unexpected results again, *don't panic*. A scientist's hypothesis often is not supported by his or her experiments. Report the truth in your conclusion. As before, state your hypothesis, but truthfully say that while your research backed up your hypothesis, your experimental results did not. Say what you expected and what actually happened. Report everything—if anything supported the hypothesis, identify it. Continue by giving reasons why you think the results did not support your original ideas. Make your explanation scientific. For example, if you think the experimental materials might have been moved during the experiment:

**Do** say: "There is a possibility that the lamp was not centered between the materials at all times. This would have resulted in the materials not receiving the same amount of light. This problem can be solved by securing the materials to the table so they are not accidentally moved during the experiment."

**Don't** say: "My little brother bumped into the box and moved it. I need to lock my door so my brother can't mess up my stuff."

Now it's time to sum up the entire project by writing a detailed report. Review the next chapter for advice on how to put together a science-fair project report.

# Chapter 7

# The Project Report

Your report is the written record of your entire project from start to finish. When read by a person unfamiliar with your project, the report should be clear and detailed enough for the reader to know exactly what you did, why you did it, what the results were, whether or not the experimental evidence supported your hypothesis, and where you got your research information. This written document is your spokesperson when you are not present to explain your project, but more than that, it documents all your work.

Much of the report will be copied from your journal. By recording everything in your journal as the project progresses, all you need to do in preparing the report is to organize and neatly copy the journal's contents. Tables, graphs, and diagrams can be neatly and colorfully prepared. If possible, use a computer to prepare some or all of these data displays.

Check with your teacher for the order and content of the report as regulated by the local fair. Generally, a project report should be typewritten, double-spaced, and bound in a folder or notebook. It should contain a title page, a table of contents, an abstract, an introduction, the experiments and data, a conclusion, a list of sources, and acknowledgments. The rest of this chapter describes these parts of a project report and gives examples based on the sample project in Chapter 6.

## TITLE PAGE

The content of the title page varies. Some fairs require that only the title of the project be centered on the page. Normally, your name would not appear on this page during judging.

Your teacher can give you the local fair's rules for this. The title should be attention getting. It should capture the theme of the project but should not be the same as the problem question. A good title for the sample project detailed in Chapter 6 is shown in Figure 7.1.

> **"Back and Forth: Winds to and from the Sea"**

*Figure 7.1   A Title Page*

## TABLE OF CONTENTS

The second page of your report is the table of contents. It should contain a list of everything in the report that follows the contents page, as shown in Figure 7.2

> **Contents**
>
> 1. Abstract
> 2. Introduction
> 3. Experiments and Data
> 4. Conclusion
> 5. Sources
> 6. Acknowledgments

*Figure 7.2   A Table of Contents*

## ABSTRACT

The abstract is a brief overview of the project. It should not be more than 1 page and should include the project title, a statement of the purpose, a hypothesis, a brief description of the procedure, and the results. There is no one way to write an abstract, but it should be brief, as shown in Figure 7.3. Often, a copy of the abstract must be submitted to the science fair officials on the day of judging, and it is a good idea to have copies available at your display. This gives judges something to refer to when making final decisions. It might also be used to prepare an introduction by a special award sponsor, so do a thorough job on this part of your report.

**1. Abstract**

**Back and Forth: Winds to and from the Sea**

The purpose of this project was to find out whether the change in temperature of sand and water affects wind direction at the beach. The experiments involved measuring how fast the temperature of water and sand changed when heated and how fast their temperature decreased when allowed to cool. This was done by recording the temperature of sand and water samples before and after heating them for 10 minutes with a desk lamp. After the lamp was turned off, the temperature of each material was again recorded after 10 minutes.

Other experiments involved measuring the temperature of the air above the heated samples of sand and water and the use of smoke to observe the direction of the air. The temperature measurements confirmed my hypothesis that there is a difference in the rate of change in temperature for sand and water, resulting in a change in wind direction at the beach. These findings lead me to believe that sea and land breezes are the result of the difference in time it takes sand and water to change temperature.

*Figure 7.3  An Abstract*

# INTRODUCTION

The introduction is a statement of your purpose, along with background information that led you to make this study. It should contain a brief statement of your hypothesis based upon your research. In other words, it should state what information or knowledge you had that led you to hypothesize the answer to the project's problem question. Make references to information or experiences that led you to choose the project's

purpose. If your teacher requires footnotes, then include one for each information source you have used. The introduction shown in Figure 7.4 does not use footnotes.

**2. Introduction**

The direction of the wind changes over land, but often it is the same for 24-hour periods and may even be the same for several days. This is not true where large bodies of water and land meet. In these areas, the wind changes direction a short time after sunset and again soon after sunrise each day.

My experience of the change of wind direction during the day and night when I was at the beach was brought to mind while reading about my project topic, the heating and cooling of water and land. Further research provided the fact that wind is the horizontal movement of air and that it moves from cool areas to warm areas. My observation while at the beach was that the wind blew toward the shore during the day and out to sea at night. This meant that the land was warmer than the water during the day, but that the water was warmer than the land at night. I reasoned that the rate that water and land change temperature must be different.

My curiosity about these land and sea breezes resulted in a project that had as its purpose to discover how the change in sand and water temperature affects the production of sea and land breezes. Based on the fact that wind direction is a result of a difference in temperature, my hypothesis was that a difference in the rate of change in the temperature of sand and water results in a change in wind direction at the beach.

*Figure 7.4  An Introduction*

# EXPERIMENTS AND DATA

Each project experiment should be listed in the experiment section of the report. Experiments should include the problem of the experiment, followed first by a list of the materials used and the amount of each, then by the procedural steps in outline or paragraph form, as shown in Figure 7.5. Note that the experiment described in Figure 7.5 investigates the exploring question "I wonder, how does the temperature of shaded and unshaded land vary?" The experiments should be written so that anyone could follow them and expect to get the same results.

## 3. Experiments and Data

**Purpose**

To determine whether structures on the shore affect sand temperature.

**Materials**

2 bulb-type thermometers

2 cups of sand

timer

**Procedure**

1. Place a thermometer in each cup so that the bulb is ¼ inch (0.63 cm) below the surface of the sand.
2. Set one cup in the shade of a tree, building, or other large structure.
3. Set the second cup in an area that will receive direct sunlight for at least 6 continuous hours.
4. Read the temperature on both thermometers. Record the temperatures in the "0 hours" section of the data chart.
5. Every hour for 6 or more hours, record the temperatures on both thermometers.

*Figure 7.5   An Experiment*

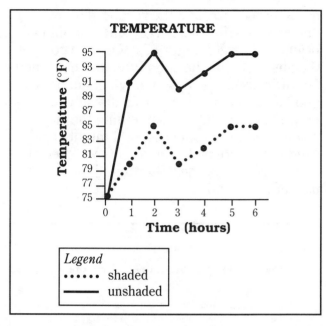

*Figure 7.7   A Line Graph*

Following each experiment, include all measurements and observations that you took during each experiment. Graphs, tables, and charts created from your data should be labeled and, if possible, colorful. Figure 7.6 shows a table and Figure 7.7 a line graph for the experiment shown in Figure 7.5. If there is a large amount of data, you may choose to put most of it in an appendix, which can be placed in a separate binder or notebook. If you do separate the material, a summary of the data should be placed in the data section of the report.

## CONCLUSION

The conclusion summarizes, in about one page or less, what you discovered based on your experimental results, as shown in Figure 7.8. The conclusion states the hypothesis and indicates whether or not the data supports it. The conclusion can also include a brief description of plans for exploring ideas for future experiments.

## SOURCES

Sources are the places where you obtained information, including all of the written materials as well as the people you have interviewed. For the written materials, write a bibliography. See "Secondary Research" in Chapter 5 for information about bibliographies. People that you interviewed should be listed separately, in alphabetical order by last name. Provide title, address, and business phone number, as shown in Figure 7.9. Do not list home addresses or phone numbers.

|  | Temperature (°F) | |
|---|---|---|
| Time (hours) | Shaded | Unshaded |
| 0 | 75 | 75 |
| 1 | 80 | 91 |
| 2 | 85 | 95 |
| 3 | 80 | 90 |
| 4 | 82 | 92 |
| 5 | 85 | 95 |
| 6 | 85 | 95 |

*Figure 7.6   A Table*

## 4. Conclusion

As stated in my hypothesis, I believe there is a difference in the rate of change in the temperature of sand and water which results in a change of wind direction at the beach. The experimental data supported my hypothesis, indicating that the rate of change of sand temperature is faster than water temperature, and that as the temperature of the sand and water changes, so does the temperature of the air that covers them. Experimental data also showed wind movement from colder to warmer areas.

Through my experiment, I discovered that large structures shade the land and cause those areas to be cooler during the day. Ideas for future experiments would include testing the temperature of the land and water at a beach, measuring the speed of air movements due to temperature changes, and testing to see whether structures on the land have any effect on this movement.

*Figure 7.8   A Project Conclusion*

## 5. Source Interviewed

Dunham, Sue
Meteorologist
215 Palm Drive
Kona, Hawaii 00008
(003) 843-0000

*Figure 7.9   An Interview Source*

# ACKNOWLEDGMENTS

Even though technically your project is to be your work alone, it is permissible to have some help. The acknowledgments is not a list of names, but a short paragraph stating the names of the people and how they helped you, as shown in Figure 7.10. Note that when listing family members or relatives, it is generally not necessary to include their names.

## 6. Acknowledgments

I would like to thank the members of my family who assisted me with this project: my mother, who proofread and typed my report, and my father and brother, who assisted in the construction of the display board.

A special note of thanks to Dr. Stella Cathey, professor of meteorology at Frances University, and to Whitney Cooper, her assistant, for their expert guidance.

*Figure 7.10   Acknowledgments*

# Chapter 8

# The Display

Your science fair display represents all the work that you have done. It should consist of a backboard, the project report, and anything that represents your project, such as models made, items studied, photographs, surveys, and the like. It must tell the story of the project in such a way that it attracts and holds the interest of the viewer. It has to be thorough, but not too crowded, so keep it simple.

The allowable size and shape of the display backboard can vary, so you will have to check the rules for your science fair. Most exhibits are allowed to be 48 inches (122 cm) wide, 30 inches (76 cm) deep, and 108 inches (274 cm) high (including the table it stands on). These are maximum measurements, so your display may be smaller than this. A three-sided backboard is usually the best way to display your work. Sturdy cardboard can be used, but heavier material is easier to work with and is less likely to be damaged during transportation to the fair. Wooden panels can be cut and hinged together. Some office supply stores sell inexpensive premade backboards. If these are not available in your area, see Appendix C for science supply companies from which you can order inexpensive pre-made backboards.

The title and other headings should be neat and large enough to be read at a distance of about 3 feet (1 m). A short title is often eye-catching. Make an effort to use six to ten words with a maximum of 50 characters in the title. Precut letters for the title and headings can be bought and glued to the backboard, or you can cut your own letters out of construction paper. You could also stencil the letters for

all the titles directly on the backboard. Self-sticking letters, of various sizes and colors, can be purchased at office supply stores. You can even use a word processor to print the title and other headings.

Some teachers have set rules about the position of the information on the backboard. The following headings are examples: Problem, Hypothesis, Procedure, Data, Results, and Conclusion. The project title should go at the top of the center panel, and the remaining material needs to be placed neatly in some order. Figure 8.1 shows one way of placing the material. The heading "Next Time," though not always required, may be included if desired. It would follow the conclusion and contain a brief description of plans for future development of the project. This information

**Figure 8.1  Example of a Good Display**

could be included in the conclusion, rather than under a separate heading.

You want a display that the judges will remember positively. So before you glue everything down, lay the board on a flat surface and arrange the materials a few different ways. This will help you decide on the most suitable and attractive presentation. Figure 8.1 shows what a good display might look like.

## HELPFUL HINTS

1. Before standing your backboard on the display table, cover the table with a colored cloth. Choose a color that matches the color scheme of the backboard. This will help to separate your project from other projects displayed on either side.

2. Place all typed material on a colored backing, such as construction paper. Leave a border of about ¼ to ½ inch (0.63 to 1.25 cm) around the edges of each piece of typed material. Use a paper cutter so that the edges will be straight.

3. Make the project title stand out by using larger letters for it and smaller letters for the headings.

4. To arrange the letters on the backboard, first lay the letters out on the board without attaching them. Then, use a yardstick (meterstick) and pencil to draw a straight, light guideline where the bottom of each letter should line up. This will help you keep the lettering straight. Before adhering everything, ask the opinion of other students, teachers, or family members.

5. If you need electricity for your project, be sure the wiring meets all safety standards.

6. Bring an emergency kit with extra letters, glue, tape, construction paper the color of the backboard, stapler, scissors, pencils, pens, touch-up paint, markers, and so forth. This kit should contain anything that you think you might need to make last-minute repairs to the display.

## DO'S AND DON'TS

**Do** use computer-generated graphs.

**Do** display photos representing the procedure and the results.

**Do** use contrasting colors.

**Do** limit the number of colors used.

**Do** display models when applicable. If possible, make the models match the color scheme of the backboard.

**Do** attach charts neatly. If there are many, place them on top of each other so that the top chart can be lifted to reveal the ones below.

**Do** balance the arrangement of materials on the backboard. This means to evenly distribute the materials on the board so that they cover about the same amount of space on each panel.

**Do** use rubber cement or double-sided tape to attach papers. White school glue causes the paper to wrinkle.

**Don't** leave large empty spaces on the backboard.

**Don't** leave the table in front of the backboard empty. Display your models (if any), report, copies of your abstract, and your journal here.

**Don't** hang electrical equipment on the backboard so that the electric cord runs down the front of the backboard.

**Don't** make the title or headings hard to read by using uneven lettering, words with letters of different colors, or disorganized placement of materials.

**Don't** hand-print the letters on the backboard.

**Don't** attach folders that fall open on the backboard.

**Don't** make mistakes in spelling words or writing formulas.

***Figure 8.2   Example of a Bad Display***

Figure 8.2 shows how *not* to set up your display.

## SAFETY

Basically, anything that is or could be hazardous to other students or the public is *prohibited* and cannot be displayed. The following is a list of things that are generally unacceptable for display. Your teacher has access to a complete list of safety rules from your local science-fair officials. Your project topic should be approved by your teacher before beginning.

This prevents you from working on an unsafe project and from wasting time on a project that would be disqualified. Models or photographs can be used instead of things that are restricted from display.

## Unacceptable for Display

1.  Live animals

2.  Microbial cultures or fungi, living or dead

3.  Animal or human parts, except for teeth, hair, nails, and dried animal bones

4.  Liquids, including water

5.  Chemicals and/or their empty containers, including caustics, acids, and household cleaners

6.  Open or concealed flames

7.  Batteries with open-top cells

8.  Combustible materials

9.  Aerosol cans of household solvents

10. Controlled substances, poisons, or drugs

11. Any equipment or device that would be hazardous to the public

12. Sharp items, such as syringes, knives, and needles

13. Gases

# Chapter 9

# Presentation and Evaluation

Your teacher may require that you give an oral presentation of your project for your class. Make it short but complete. Presenting in front of your classmates may be the hardest part of the project. You want to do your best, so prepare and practice, practice, practice. If possible, tape your practice presentation on a tape recorder or have someone videotape you. Review the tape and/or video and evaluate yourself. Review your notes and practice again.

Practicing an oral presentation will also be helpful for the science fair itself. The judges give points for how clearly you are able to discuss the project and explain its purpose, procedure, results, and conclusion. The display should be organized so that it explains everything, but your ability to discuss your project and answer the questions of the judges convinces them that you did the work and understand what you have done. Practice a speech in front of friends, and invite them to ask questions. If you do not know the answer to a question, never guess or make up an answer or just say, "I don't know." Instead, say that you did not discover that answer during your research, and then offer other information that you found of interest about the project. Be proud of the project and approach the judges with enthusiasm about your work.

You can decide on how best to dress for a class presentation, but for the local fair, it is wise to make a special effort to look nice. You are representing your work. In effect, you are acting as a salesperson for your project, and you want to present the very best image possible. Your appearance shows how much personal pride you have in yourself, and that is the first step in introducing your product, your science project.

## JUDGING INFORMATION

Most fairs have similar point systems for judging a science fair project, but you may be better prepared by understanding that judges generally start by thinking that each student's project is average. Then, he or she adds or subtracts points from that. A student should receive more points for accomplishing the following:

1. Project Objectives
   - Presenting original ideas
   - Stating the problem clearly
   - Defining the variables and using controls
   - Relating background reading to the problem

2. Project Skills
   - Being knowledgeable about equipment used
   - Performing the experiments with little or no assistance except as required for safety
   - Demonstrating the skills required to do all the work necessary to obtain the data reported

3. Data Collection
   - Using a journal to collect data and research
   - Repeating the experiment to verify the results
   - Spending an appropriate amount of time to complete the project

**4.** Data Interpretation

- Using tables, graphs, and illustrations in interpreting data
- Using research to interpret data collected
- Collecting enough data to make a conclusion
- Using only data collected to make a conclusion

**5.** Project Presentation (Written Materials/Interview/Display)

- Having a complete and comprehensive report
- Answering questions accurately
- Using the display during oral presentation
- Justifying conclusions on the basis of experimental data
- Summarizing what was learned
- Presenting a display that shows creative ability and originality
- Presenting an attractive and interesting display

## DO'S AND DON'TS AT THE FAIR

**Do** bring activities, such as puzzles to work on or a book to read, to keep yourself occupied at your booth. There may be a lengthy wait before the first judge arrives, and even between judges.

**Do** become acquainted with your neighboring presenters. Be friendly and courteous.

**Do** ask neighboring presenters about their projects, and tell them about yours if they express interest. These conversations pass time and help relieve nervous tension that can build when one is waiting to be evaluated. You may also discover techniques for research that you can use for next year's project.

**Do** have fun.

**Don't** laugh or talk loud. This may affect the person nearby who is being judged.

**Don't** forget that you are an ambassador for your school. This means that your attitude and behavior influence how people at the fair think about you and the students at your school.

# II

# 50 SCIENCE FAIR PROJECT IDEAS

# Astronomy

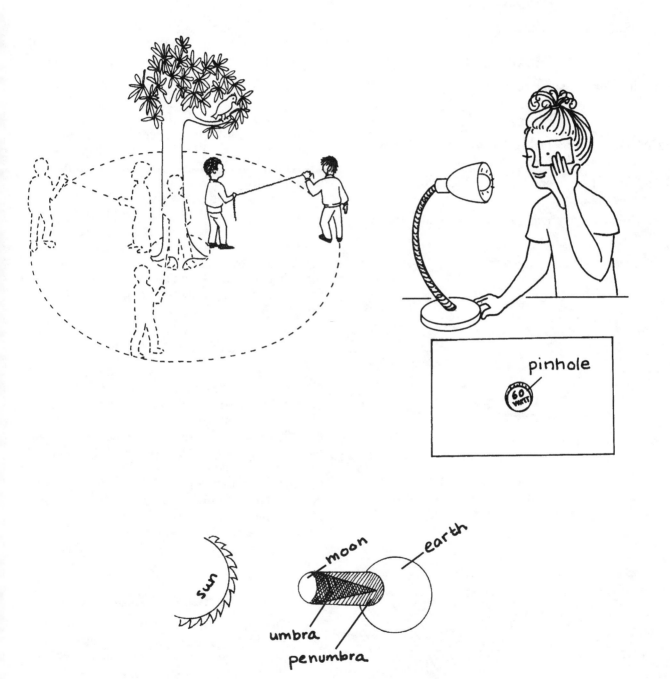

pinhole

60 WATT

sun

moon

earth

umbra

penumbra

# Blackout

## PROBLEM

*What causes a solar eclipse?*

## Materials

dime or any small coin

## Procedure

*CAUTION: Never look at the sun directly, because it can permanently damage your eyes.*

1. Close one eye and look at a distant tree with your open eye.

2. Hold the coin near and to the side of your open eye.

3. Move the coin until it is in front of your open eye and about even with the end of your nose.

## Results

As the coin nears the front of your face, it comes between your eye and the tree. Less of the tree is seen, until finally all or most of the tree is no longer visible.

## Why?

In this experiment, the tree represents the sun; the dime, the moon; and your eye, the earth. The coin is smaller than the tree, just as the moon is smaller than the sun, but they are both able to block out light and cast a shadow. The closer they are to the observer, the more light they block. The sun is so far away that it looks like a disk in the sky. The moon is close to the earth; thus, it can block out the sun's light when it passes directly between the sun and the earth. The blocking of the sun's light by the moon is called a **solar eclipse**.

## LET'S EXPLORE

Since the moon **revolves** (moves in a curved path around an object) around the earth about once a month, why don't eclipses happen each month? Solar eclipses occur when the moon passes directly between the sun and the earth. Repeat the experiment, changing the location of the coin. Hold the coin up so that it is slightly above your eye, then move it down so that it is slightly below your eye. Notice that the coin only blocks your view of the tree when the tree, coin, and your eye are in line with each other. A solar eclipse occurs only when the sun, moon, and earth are in line with each other.

## SHOW TIME!

1a. Determine why the whole earth is not darkened by a solar eclipse. Use a compass to draw a 20-inch (50-cm)-diameter circle in the center of a poster board. Label the circle "Earth." Place the poster board on the ground in a sunny area outdoors. Stick a lemon-sized ball of clay on the eraser end of a pencil. The clay ball represents the moon. Push the point of the pencil through the center of the circle and into the ground so that the pencil stands upright. Observe the size of the shadow cast by the clay ball and the amount of the circle that it covers. If the shadow of the ball falls outside the circle, push the pencil farther into the ground. The shadow of the moon, like that of the clay ball, covers only a small portion of the earth.

**b.** Does the shadow cast by the moon during a solar eclipse stay in one place on the earth? Repeat the previous experiment, making a mark on the poster board in the center of the clay ball's shadow. Mark the poster board every 30 minutes six or more times during the day. Use your results and the fact that the earth **rotates** (turns on its axis) to determine whether the shadow of the moon falls on different areas during a solar eclipse. Use diagrams to create a display to represent the results.

**2.** During a total solar eclipse, the moon blocks the glaring light from the sun's **photosphere** (the visible surface of the sun), allowing the less intense layer of glowing gas around the sun, called the **corona**, to be studied. Demonstrate this by asking an adult to make a pinhole in the center of an index card with the point of a compass. Close one eye and hold the card over your open eye. Look through the pinhole in the card at the glowing bulb in a lamp. The print on the outside of the bulb can be read when looking through the pinhole. *CAUTION: Do not look at the sun through the pinhole.*

**3.** Determine why some areas of the moon's shadow are darker than others during a solar eclipse by laying a sheet of typing

paper on a table. Position a desk lamp about 14 inches (35 cm) from the paper. Place your hand between the light and the paper about 1 inch (2.5 cm) above the paper. Notice that the shadow of your hand is darker in the center than on the outside. Draw and display a diagram of a solar eclipse. Label the two parts of the shadow: the **umbra** (the darker inner part of a shadow) and the **penumbra** (the lighter outer part of a shadow).

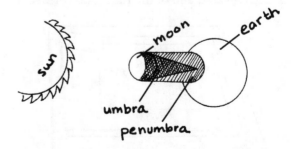

## CHECK IT OUT!

An eclipse of the moon is called a *lunar eclipse*. What is the position of the sun, moon, and earth during a lunar eclipse? Find out more about solar and lunar eclipses. What is an annular eclipse? Which type of eclipse occurs more often?

# Circling

## PROBLEM

*What keeps a satellite in orbit around a planet?*

## Materials

cookie sheet with raised sides
cardboard tube from a toilet tissue roll
masking tape
sheet of typing paper
cup
tap water
red food coloring
spoon
marble
modeling clay

## Procedure

1. Lay the cookie sheet on a table.

2. Place the cardboard tube in one corner of the cookie sheet so that one end of the tube rests on the rim of one short side of the pan.

3. Secure the raised end of the tube to the rim of the pan with tape.

4. Lay the paper in the pan so that the untaped end of the tube rests on the edge of the paper.

5. Fill the cup about one-fourth full with water and add 10 drops of food coloring. Stir.

6. Wet the marble with the colored water, place it in the elevated end of the tube, and release it.

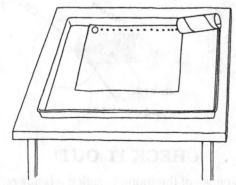

7. Prop up the long side of the pan nearest the tube about 1 inch (2.5 cm) by placing 2 lumps of clay under both corners of the long side.

8. Again, wet the marble, place it in the tube, and release it.

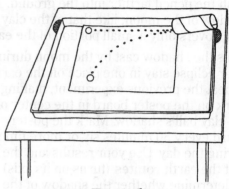

## Results

Spots of red water mark the two paths of the marble. The path across the level pan is straight, while the path across the raised pan is curved.

## Why?

Gravity (the force pulling things toward the center of the earth) pulls the marble down the elevated tube and holds the marble on the flat pan as it rolls forward in a straight line. On the elevated pan, the marble moves forward as it leaves the raised tube, but the earth's gravity tries to pull the marble down toward the lower end of the pan. The combination of the marble's forward motion and the downward pull of gravity causes the marble to move in a curved path. The path of a **satellite** (a celestial body that revolves about another celestial body), like that of the marble on the elevated pan, curves because its forward speed and the planet's gravity pull it down toward the planet. Without gravity, satellites would move in a straight path, and without forward speed, gravity would pull the satellite into the planet. The curved path that a satellite traces around a planet is called an **orbit**.

## LET'S EXPLORE

1. How would an increase in forward speed affect the orbit of a satellite? Repeat the experiment, using a different sheet of paper and a lump of clay to further raise the elevated end of the tube.

2. How would an increase in gravity affect the path of a satellite? While gravity does not change greatly around a given planet, the results of increasing the pan's elevation can be used to simulate the effect on satellites orbiting different planets with stronger gravity. Repeat the original experiment, using a different sheet of paper and more clay to increase the elevation of the pan.

3. With an increase in gravity, would an increase in forward speed send the marble on the same curved path as in the original experiment? On a different sheet of paper, trace the curved path made by the marble in the original experiment, and place the tracing in the pan. Repeat the previous experiment, increasing the height of the elevated end of the tube. **Science Fair Hint:** Use the papers with red water–marked paths from each experiment as part of a science fair display.

## SHOW TIME!

How can some satellites appear to stay in one spot above the earth? Determine this by using a tree or other object outdoors to represent the Earth. Ask a helper to hold one end of a rope about 3 yards (3 m) long as you hold on to the other end. Have your helper stand near the tree. Together, walk at a pace around the tree that keeps the rope taut and in a straight line between you as you trace imaginary circles around the tree. Your helper will trace a small circle while you will trace a larger circle around the tree. The distance around the outer circle is greater than that of the circle near the tree. Thus, you must walk faster than your helper in order to trace the larger circle at the same time that your helper traces the smaller circle. A satellite that stays above one spot on the earth must travel at a speed that gives it an **orbital period** (the time required to complete one orbit) of 24 hours, the same as that of the earth; the satellite thus appears to remain stationary above the earth.

## CHECK IT OUT!

Satellites that remain above one spot on the earth are called *geostationary satellites*. Find out more about these orbiting craft. What is their height above the earth? What is their speed? What is the purpose of these satellites? For information about geostationary satellites, see pages 72–73 in *Janice VanCleave's Astronomy for Every Kid* (New York: Wiley, 1991).

# Biology

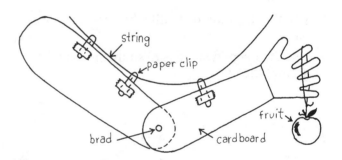

string

paper clip

brad

cardboard

fruit

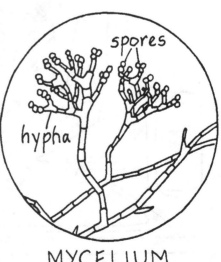

spores

hypha

MYCELIUM

# Modified

### PROBLEM

*What are the different parts of a fingernail?*

### Materials

soap
tap water
paper towel
magnifying lens

### Procedure

1. Wash your hands with soap and water.
2. Dry your hands with the paper towel.
3. Use the magnifying lens to examine your fingernails.
4. Use the diagram to identify the parts of your nails.
5. Use the magnifying lens to study the skin around the nails.

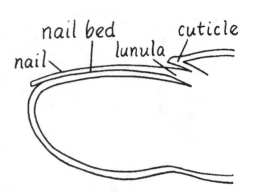

### Results

The part of the nail that covers the finger is pink; the part that extends past the end of the finger looks white. There is often a whitish, half-moon–shaped area near the base of the nail. Some nails have white spots. The skin around the nail often looks dry and scaly.

## Why?

Your fingernails are simply made up of skin **cells** (the smallest units or building blocks of all living things) that have been pressed together tightly to form a thin, rigid plate. The **nail bed** is the pink, fleshy area beneath the nail that provides a smooth surface for the nail to grow across, and its pink color is caused by the rich supply of blood beneath it. All the new growth of a nail takes place beneath the whitish, half-moon–shaped area known as the **lunula**. The ridges and bumps on a nail are due to uneven growth of the nail at the **nail root** (the area beneath the lunula). White, irregularly shaped flecks in the nail are bubbles of air trapped between the cell layers. The **cuticle** is dead skin around the base and sides of the fingernails.

## TRY IT WITH A MICROSCOPE

### Microscope Procedure

1. If you do not have a nail that extends past the end of your finger, find a helper who does.
2. Place the finger with the longest nail on the stage of the microscope.
3. Position a desk lamp so that the nail is brightly lit from above.
4. Under low power, study the structure of the top surface of the tip of the nail.
5. Paint the end of the nail with a thin layer of red fingernail polish.
6. Again, observe the nail tip under low power.

### Microscope Results

The nail's surface varies from one individual to the next, but no one's nails are smooth. The red polish aids in observing the variations or roughness in the nail's surface.

### LET'S EXPLORE

Do toenails look the same as fingernails? Repeat the original experiment observing toenails instead of fingernails. Since it is difficult to

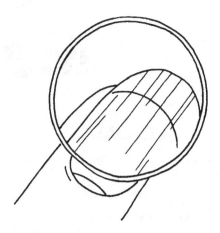

observe your own toenails, use the toenails of a helper. **Science Fair Hint:** Make diagrams of nails as viewed with your unaided eye and as viewed through the magnifying lens and microscope. Describe the nails and label the structural parts. Use the diagrams as part of a project display.

### SHOW TIME!

Like fingernails, hair is made up of modified skin cells. A **pigment** (coloring matter) called **melanin** in the hair shaft determines the actual color of the hair. Find out why some hair turns gray or white. Collect samples of hair from a person who has both naturally colored and gray hair. Observe the hair samples with a magnifying lens or a microscope. Display the samples in a sealed plastic bag with diagrams of their magnified appearance, along with an explanation of the differences in color.

### CHECK IT OUT!

Temperature seems to affect the growth rate of nails: Nails grow faster in the summer months than during the winter. Use a science encyclopedia to find out more about fingernails. What is the average rate of growth for nails? Do nails grow at different rates on the same hand? Do nails on the right hand grow at a different rate from those on the left hand? Do toenails grow at the same rate as fingernails?

# Human Machine

**4**

## PROBLEM

*What kind of simple machine is your forearm?*

## Materials

plastic bucket with handle

## Procedure

1. Place your elbow on a table so that your forearm lies flat and your hand extends straight out over the table's edge. The palm of your hand should be face up.
2. Place the handle of the bucket in the hand of your extended arm.
3. Lift your forearm, but do not raise your elbow from the table.

## Results

As the height of your forearm above the table increases, the height of the bucket also increases.

## Why?

A **lever** is a simple machine, consisting of a rigid bar and a fixed point of rotation called a **fulcrum**, that is used to lift or move things. In a **third-class lever**, such as your forearm, the **effort force** (the force that you apply) is between the fulcrum and the **load** (the object being lifted or moved by a machine), in this case, your hand and the bucket. As you raise your forearm, it rotates at the elbow, and thus your elbow acts as a fulcrum. The weight of your hand plus the weight of the bucket make up the **resistance force** (the weight of the load). The effort force needed to lift the load is applied by the muscles in the arm. The total amount of resistance that you can lift depends on the strength of these muscles. As in all third-class levers, the effort force lies between the fulcrum and the load, making the **effort arm** (the distance from the effort force to the fulcrum) shorter than the **resistance arm** (the distance from the load to the fulcrum of a lever).

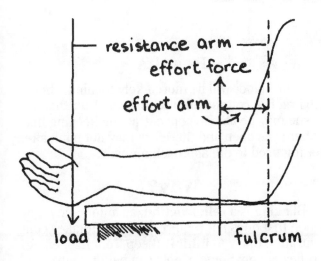

## LET'S EXPLORE

1. The distance from the elbow to the point where the muscles are attached to the bones of the forearm is the effort arm. The distance from the palm of the hand to the elbow is the resistance arm. Would increasing the length of the resistance arm affect the effort needed to raise the load? Repeat the experiment twice, holding a yardstick (meterstick) in your hand. First, hang the bucket on the stick near your hand. Then, hang the bucket on the far end of the stick.

2a. What is the greatest load that you can lift using your forearm as a third-class lever? Repeat the original experiment, asking a helper to place heavy objects, such as rocks, in the bucket one at a time until you can barely lift the load. Use a food scale to measure the weight of the bucket.

b. Would increasing the resistance arm affect the results? Repeat the previous experiment, using the yardstick (meterstick) as in Let's Explore 1.

## SHOW TIME!

1. The amount by which a machine increases an effort force is its **mechanical advantage**

(MA). If the MA for your forearm is 4, then the resistance force is 4 times the effort force applied by your arm. Use this average MA to determine the effort force needed to lift the empty bucket.

- First, calculate the resistance force using these steps:

  a. Measure and record the weight of the bucket.

  b. Keeping your elbow on the table, place your hand on the food scale and record its weight.

  c. Calculate the total resistance force by adding the weight of the bucket and your hand.

- Then, divide the resistance force by 4.

2. Construct a cardboard model of a forearm as in the diagram. Label and use the model as part of a project display to demonstrate a third-class lever. Label the parts of the lever and include a short explanation of how muscles work.

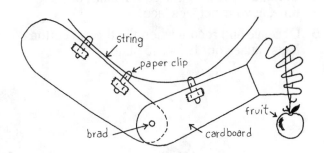

## CHECK IT OUT!

Your lower jaw, like your forearm, acts as a third-class lever. Find out more about how the human body compares to simple machines. An experiment that uses your fingers to demonstrate another kind of lever can be found on pages 120–121 of *Janice VanCleave's Physics for Every Kid* (New York: Wiley, 1991).

# 5

# Blinkers

## PROBLEM

*What kind of behavior is blinking?*

## Materials

sheet of transparent plastic wrap
10 cotton balls
helper

## Procedure

*CAUTION: Do not substitute materials. It would be unsafe to use anything other than cotton balls.*

1. Have your helper hold the plastic wrap in front of his or her face.
2. Stand about 1 yard (1 m) away from your helper.
3. Without warning, throw a cotton ball directly at your helper's face. The cotton ball will be stopped by the plastic wrap.
4. Continue throwing the cotton balls, one at a time, at your helper's face.
5. Observe and record when the thrown cotton balls cause your helper to blink.

## Results

Your helper will be more likely to blink when the first few cotton balls are thrown. After that, he or she may be able to concentrate on keeping his or her eyes open and therefore may not blink after getting used to the approaching balls.

## Why?

Blinking is a **reflex action**, an automatic action that does not require thinking. It takes concentration to try to **inhibit** (keep from happening) a reflex action. Some people can better control the blinking response if they are aware that the **stimuli** (things that cause a response—the thrown cotton balls in this experiment) are coming. Animals with eyelids behave the same way. If an unexpected object suddenly approaches, their eyelids blink automatically. This involuntary movement is due to **sensory** (having to do with the senses: sight, hearing, taste, touch, and smell) cells in the eye sending a message to a control center in the spine. From the spine, the instructions to close the eyes for protection are immediately relayed to the eye muscles, resulting in the blinking action.

## LET'S EXPLORE

Would the reflex response be affected if the cotton balls came unexpectedly from different directions? Determine this by repeating the experiment, but have two people throw cotton balls at odd times from different directions at a person shielding his or her face with a sheet of plastic wrap. **Science Fair Hint:** Use photographs of this experiment as part of a project display, along with a summary of the results.

## SHOW TIME!

1. Cats have whiskers on their faces which are attached to nerves in the skin. These hairs respond to the slightest touch and help cats feel their way through small spaces. Test the sensitivity of human hair by asking a helper to look away as you gently move your hand back and forth against the ends of hairs on your helper's arm. Did your helper feel the movements? Find out more about how animals use hair to respond to their environment.

2. Do **organisms** (living things) other than **mammals** (warm-blooded, hairy animals with backbones) have reflex actions? Place several earthworms on a moist paper towel, and record their response to being touched with the end of a string. Use a biology text to find out about an earthworm's nervous system and how it responds to stimuli, such as touch. Photographs along with a summary of the responses can be displayed. *NOTE: Approval for using living organisms in your science fair project may be needed. Check with your teacher before beginning this experiment. Upon completion of the experiment, return the worms to their natural environment.*

3. What are some other common reflex actions in humans? Display diagrams showing reflex actions that happen as a result of

   a. being startled

   b. tapping the soft spot on the knee, below the kneecap

   c. touching something sharp, like a tack

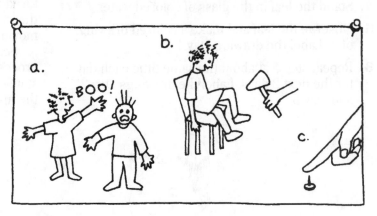

## CHECK IT OUT!

Reflex action is an example of simple *innate* (inborn) animal behavior. Another example of reflex action is seen when animals jerk away from heat before actually feeling the pain. Find out about the protective short-circuit path taken by nerve impulses that produces a reflex action. Display a diagram along with your explanation of the movement of the nerve impulses.

# 6

# Climbers

## PROBLEM

*How does water move through a leaf?*

### Materials

juice glass
tap water
red food coloring
scissors
large tree leaf, such as an oak leaf
crayons or colored markers
3 sheets of typing paper

### Procedure

1. Fill the glass about one-fourth full with water.

2. Add enough food coloring to make the water a deep red color.

3. Cut across the end of the leaf's stem.

4. Stand the leaf in the glass of colored water.

5. Observe the leaf and make a colored drawing of it. Label the drawing Day 1.

6. Repeat step 5 at about the same time each day for the next 2 days. Label the drawings Day 2 and Day 3.

### Results

The red color moves slowly through the leaf, first following the pattern made by the leaf's **veins** (conducting structures in leaves) and then throughout the rest of the leaf.

### Why?

The leaf is part of a vascular plant. A **vascular plant** has a **vascular system** containing bundles of **vascular tubes**, which transport **sap** (plant liquid). A leaf's **veins** are made up of bundles of vascular tubes. There are two types of vascular tubes: xylem tubes and phloem tubes. **Xylem tubes** transport sap containing water and minerals upward from the roots through the plant. The xylem tubes also provide support for the plant because their walls are thick. **Phloem tubes** transport sap containing water and food manufactured in the plant's leaves throughout the plant. In this activity, you saw the results of colored water moving through xylem tubes.

Scientists believe that **transpiration** (a process by which **water vapor**—water in the gas state— is lost through leaves) is responsible for the upward movement of water through xylem

tubes against the pull of gravity. Xylem tubes from the roots to the leaves are believed to be filled with sap, which is mostly water. Some of the water in xylem tubes **evaporates** (changes from a liquid to a gas due to an addition of heat energy) during transpiration. As water is lost from the xylem tubes, the column of sap in the tube is pulled upward. This is because water **molecules** (the smallest particles of a substance that retain the properties of the substance) hold tightly to each other. As the water molecules in the xylem tubes move upward, water from the soil is pulled into the roots.

## LET'S EXPLORE

1. Will water move the same way through a vascular plant that has a longer stem? Repeat the experiment, using a pale stalk of celery with pale leaves. (These can be found in the center of a celery bunch.)

2. How do changes in the rate at which water evaporates from leaves affect the speed at which water moves through xylem tubes? Repeat the previous experiment, preparing 3 stalks of celery in 3 glasses. Ask an adult to cut the bottom from a 2-liter soda bottle. Cover one of the glasses with the bottle, as shown, and set the second glass next to the bottle. Set the third glass at a distance from the other glasses and in front of a blowing fan. *NOTE: A dry, windy environment increases evaporation.* Observe the celery stalks and leaves in each glass every 15 minutes for 1 hour and then as often as possible for 8 to 10 hours. **Science Fair Hint:** Display drawings of the results.

## SHOW TIME!

**1a.** Demonstrate transpiration by placing a clear plastic bag over a group of leaves at the end of a stem of a tree or bush. (Do not cut or break the stem off the plant.) Secure the bag to the stem by wrapping tape around the open end of the bag. Observe the contents of the bag as often as possible for 2 to 3 days.

**b.** Does the amount of transpiration vary in different plants? Repeat the previous experiment, placing the bag over the leaves of two to three different types of plant. Try to have each bag contain about the same amount of leaf surface area. Compare the results of each bag.

**2.** As water moves into a cell, pressure builds up inside the cell. This internal pressure is called **turgor pressure**. The **turgidity** of a cell is its firmness due to turgor pressure. A decrease in turgidity causes plant stems to **wilt** (become limp). Demonstrate wilting by placing a fresh stalk of celery with high turgidity in an empty glass. Evaluate the turgidity of the celery by trying to bend the stalk. Test the turgidity again after 24 hours.

## CHECK IT OUT!

When a plant transpires more water than it absorbs, *temporary wilting* occurs. *Permanent wilting* occurs when the water supply is exhausted or the plant's roots are damaged. Find out more about the wilting of plants. Does temporary wilting damage plants?

# 7

# Inside and Out

## PROBLEM

*What's on the outside of a pinto bean?*

### Materials

4 to 6 dry pinto beans
coffee cup
ruler
tap water
timer
paper towel

### Procedure

1. Place the beans in the cup and cover them with about 2 inches (5 cm) of water.

2. Soak the beans for 24 hours.

3. After 24 hours, take the beans out of the cup and place them on the paper towel to absorb the excess water.

4. Use your fingernail to remove the outer covering from one of the beans. Observe the color and thickness of the covering.

*NOTE: Keep the remaining beans for the next two experiments.*

### Results

The outside of the bean consists of a thin outer coat that is light brown with irregularly shaped dark spots.

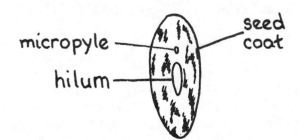

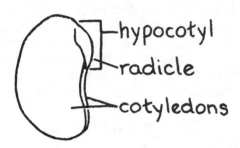

### Why?

A bean is a **seed**, inside of which is an **embryo** (an organism in its earliest stage of development) surrounded by a stored food supply. The seed is covered by a protective outer covering called the **seed coat**, which protects the inside of the seed from insects, disease, and damage. The seed coat of the pinto bean has a light-colored, oval-shaped scar called the **hilum** and a small dot at one end of the hilum called the **micropyle**.

### LET'S EXPLORE

1. What's under the seed coat of a pinto bean? Use one of the soaked pinto beans from the experiment. Remove the seed coat to reveal a white structure with two separate halves connected at a single spot at the top. The two halves are **cotyledons**, or seed leaves, which are simple leaves that store food for the developing plant embryo. (Plants with two cotyledons are called **dicotyledons** or **dicots.**) Extending from the connecting spot is a beak-shaped structure called the **hypocotyl**. The hypocotyl is the part of the plant embryo that develops into roots and, very often, the lower stem. The tip of the hypocotyl, called the **radicle**, develops into roots. Use a magnifying lens to examine these parts. Repeat the procedure, using 3 or 4 more beans.

2. What's inside a pinto bean? Use the soaked beans from the original experiment. Remove

the seed coat and gently pry the cotyledons open with your fingernail, then spread them apart. Be careful not to break the hypocotyl. Use a magnifying lens to study the parts of the embryo inside. Use the diagram to identify the following parts of the **embryonic** (undeveloped) **shoot** (the part of a plant that grows above ground):

- **epicotyl**   The part of a plant embryo, located above the hypocotyl, that develops into the plant's stem, leaves, flowers, and fruit.

- **plumule**   The part of a plant embryo, located at the tip of the embryonic shoot, that consists of several tiny, immature leaves that at maturity form the first true leaves.

**Science Fair Hint:** Prepare and display a labeled drawing of the outside and inside of the bean.

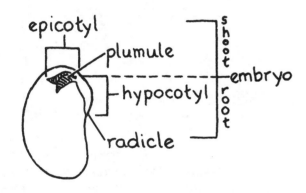

**3.** What's inside other beans? Repeat the previous experiment using different beans, such as lima and kidney.

## SHOW TIME!

**1a.** Use a magnifying lens to study the hilum and micropyle on a pinto bean. A biology text can be used to find out how the features formed during the development of the seed.

**b.** Repeat the previous experiment, using other beans.

**2.** During germination (the beginning of growth or development) of a pinto bean, which part of the embryo develops first?

Soak 30 to 40 beans in 1 cup (250 ml) of water. *NOTE: You'll need the extra beans in case some of the embryos are damaged.* Fold a paper towel in half twice and place it on a piece of aluminum foil that is about 12 inches (30 cm) square. Wet the towel with water. Place all but 3 of the soaked beans on the wet paper towel. Fold the aluminum foil over the beans to keep them moist. Open the 3 reserved beans and use a magnifying lens to observe their embryo parts. Make a diagram showing the cotyledons and the attached embryo. The diagram should indicate the size of the cotyledon and the embryo parts. Each day for 7 days, remove 3 beans from the foil and observe their embryos. Make another diagram showing size and location of the embryo in the cotyledon. Create and display a poster using the drawings to show the development of the bean embryo.

## CHECK IT OUT!

The seed coats of different seeds vary in color, thickness, and texture. Sometimes the seed coat is smooth and paper-thin, like that of a pinto bean. A coconut's seed coat, however, is rough, thick, and hard. A seed cannot develop into a plant until the seed coat is broken. Find out how the seed coats of different seeds are broken. For more information about the breaking of seed coats, see Chapter 10, "Attractive," in *Janice VanCleave's Plants* (New York: Wiley, 1997).

# 8 Light Seekers

## PROBLEM

*How do grass seedlings respond to light?*

## Materials

scissors
ruler
cardboard box about 18 × 12 × 9 inches
   (45 × 30 × 22.5 cm)
9-ounce (270-ml) paper cup
potting soil
½ teaspoon (2.5 ml) grass seeds, such as rye,
   oat, or wheat
saucer
pencil
tap water
masking tape
sponge
flashlight
adult helper

## Procedure

1. Ask an adult to cut a 3-inch (7.5-cm)-square opening in the center and near the top of one side of the box.

2. Fill the cup with potting soil to within 2 inches (5 cm) of the top.

3. Sprinkle the grass seeds over the surface of the soil.

4. Cover the seeds with about 1 inch (2.5 cm) of soil.

5. Hold the cup above the saucer and use the pencil to punch two opposite holes in the bottom edge of the cup.

6. Set the cup in the saucer.

7. Moisten the soil with water.

8. Put the cup and saucer inside the cardboard box on the side opposite the opening in the side of the box.

9. Close the box and seal all cracks in the box with tape to allow light to enter only through the opening.

10. Place the box near a window so that the opening in the box faces the window.

11. Allow the cup to remain undisturbed for 21 days. Keep the soil moist throughout the experiment by wetting the sponge with water and inserting it through the opening in the box. Squeeze the water from the sponge into the cup, being careful not to disturb the growing plants.

12. Make daily observations by turning the box around and shining the flashlight into the opening in the box. Record the growth of the grass seeds above the surface of the soil. After observing, be sure to return the box to its original position with the opening facing the window.

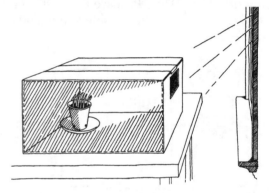

*NOTE: Determine the average number of hours of sunlight the box receives during the day by counting the hours between sunrise and sunset on the eleventh day of the experiment. This information will be needed for a later experiment.*

## Results

The first signs of growth appear in 4 to 6 days, when straight, tubelike structures break through the soil and bend toward the opening in the box. After several more days, a single leaf breaks through the end of the each tube. The tubes and leaves bend toward the opening.

## Why?

Grass seeds are monocotyledons or **monocots** (a flowering plant having one cotyledon). The tubelike structure that breaks through the soil is the **coleoptile**, a structure in grass seeds that covers and protects the tip of the embryonic shoot. A short time after the coleoptile breaks through the surface of the soil, it stops growing, and the tip of the first leaf of the shoot breaks through.

The coleoptile and the leaf then bend toward the light because of the plant chemical **auxin**. Auxin moves away from a light source. When a plant is unevenly lit, auxin builds up on the shaded side of the stem, causing the cells on that side of the plant to grow longer. As a result, the plant bends toward the light. The growth response of plants to light is a plant behavior called **phototropism**.

## LET'S EXPLORE

1. Would artificial light affect the results? Repeat the experiment, but instead of putting the box near a window, place a desk lamp about 12 inches (30 cm) in front of the opening in the box. Turn the lamp on each day for the number of hours you calculate to be the average number of hours of sunlight the box received each day in the original experiment.

2. Do other monocot **seedlings** (young plants grown from seeds) behave the same way? Repeat the original experiment using corn kernels. A corn kernel contains the seed of a monocot.

3. How do dicot seedlings respond to natural light? Repeat the original experiment, using dicot seeds, such as pinto beans. Keep the seedlings for the following experiment. **Science Fair Hint:** Create and display diagrams to represent the results of each experiment.

## SHOW TIME!

1. How far will plant stems bend in response to light? Place the bean seedlings from the previous experiment in a tall box that has an opening near the bottom of one side. Stand the cup of seedlings on an object, such as a jar, so that the plants touch the inside top of the box. Seal all cracks in the box with tape. Every 7 days for a total of 21 days, open the box and observe the position of the stems and leaves of the plants. While observing the plants, moisten the soil if it is dry. Take photographs and make diagrams of the plants to represent the results.

2. **Positive phototropism** is growth toward light, and **negative phototropism** is growth away from light. Do the stems and leaves of mature plants exhibit positive phototropism or negative phototropism? With an adult's permission, obtain a small houseplant. Ask the adult to remove the top and one side of a box that is as tall as the plant. Keep the top of the box to use as a cover. Place the plant in the box. Tape a string across the top of the cutaway side of the box. Tape a ruler across the top of an adjacent (neighboring) side of the box so that one end of the ruler meets one end of the string. Put the box next to a window so that the cutaway side faces the window. Place the cover over the top of the box. Remove the cover and take photographs of the plant from the same position every day for 21 days. Measure and record the distance of the leaves from the string each day to determine phototropism. Repeat using a different kind of plant.

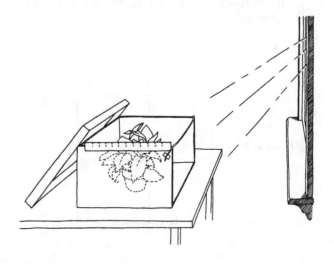

# Sampling

## PROBLEM

*How can an ecology sampling plot be prepared?*

## Materials

compass
measuring tape
9 sharpened pencils
scissors
70 feet (21 m) of cord

## Procedure

1. Select a study area that has a variety of plant life. This can be a forest, an open field, or the yard around your home.
2. Use the compass to find north.
3. With the measuring tape, measure an area 10 feet (3 m) square, the sides of which face the compass directions (N, S, E, and W).
4. At each of the four corners of the plot, drive a pencil into the ground, leaving about 5 inches (12.5 cm) of the pencil above ground.
5. Use the measuring tape to divide each side of the plot into 5-foot (1.5-m) sections.
6. Drive a pencil into the ground at each 5-foot (1.5-m) interval along all sides of the plot. Drive a pencil into the ground at the center of the plot.
7. Using scissors and cord to join adjacent (neighboring) pencils, divide the plot into four equal subplots.

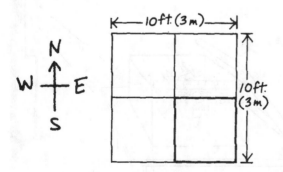

## Results

A plot of ground is selected, measured, and subdivided as a sampling plot for an ecosystem. An **ecosystem** is a distinct area that combines **biotic** (living) communities and the **abiotic** (non-living) environments with which they interact.

## Why?

It would be difficult if not impossible to study every part of an ecosystem. The sampling plot provides a small part of an ecosystem that can be studied thoroughly. Separate information taken from each subplot and studied as a whole provides a clear picture of the **ecological community** (interaction of living organisms with their environment) within the entire plot. This information gives you clues to the surrounding ecosystem. However, for more accurate information, you must follow the example of **ecologists** (scientists who study organisms and their environment) and study more plots. These plots should be selected randomly from different locations within the ecosystem.

## LET'S EXPLORE

Are the abiotic features (soil, walkways, rocks, litter, temperature, and the like) and biotic features (plants, animals, and insects) the same in each subplot? Make a sketch of each subplot, numbering the plots from 1 to 4. Design a way to note the number and size of prominent features, such as rocks, trees, trails, areas of **erosion** (the wearing away of the earth's surface, usually by wind or water), open areas, animals, and the like. Use a thermometer to determine the temperature in different locations of each subplot. **Science Fair Hint:** Use the sketches as part of a project display.

## SHOW TIME!

1. Collect leaf samples from the plants in your plot. Using plant field guides, identify each type of plant present. Display photographs of the plants along with preserved samples. Plants can be preserved by drying, using a method such as one of the following three.

5 ft. (1.5 m)

5 ft. (1.5 m)

- Tie the stems of a bunch of plants together and hang them upside down.

- Dry whole flowers by placing them in a jar that is 1 to 2 inches (1.25 to 2.5 cm) larger on the top, bottom, and sides than the plant. First, pour a 1- to 2-inch (1.25- to 2.5-cm) layer of borax powder in the jar. Then, place the plant in the jar and fill the jar with borax. Allow the jar to remain undisturbed for 1 week. Remove the flower and gently shake the borax powder off the petals. One way of displaying these dried plants is to place one or more plants inside a small clear plastic jar and seal the jar with a lid. Label the jar with the name of the plant(s). The jar can be held and rotated to see all the sides of the plant without injuring it.

- Another method of preserving plants is to press them. Prepare a pressed plant by placing several sheets of newspaper on a table that will not be needed for a while. Place a sheet of white construction paper in the center of the newspapers. Arrange a plant on the construction paper so that the leaves and flower(s) are faceup. Use your fingers to gently press each plant part into position. Cover the plant with a second sheet of white construction paper. Cover the paper with several sheets of newspaper. Stack books on top of the newspaper. After 3 to 4 weeks, remove the books and papers. The pressed plant should be stuck to the bottom sheet of

paper, but if not, add a drop of glue to the back of the flowers, leaves, and stems to secure them to the paper.

2. Collect insects from your plot. Make an insect net by bending a coat hanger into a hoop. Attach to the hoop a mesh laundry bag (or use a regular size pillowcase instead). Secure one end of the hoop to a broom handle. Walk across subplot 1 in a straight line, sweeping the net back and forth as you walk. Close the net. Empty the contents of the net into a jar and cover with a knee-high stocking. Label the jar Subplot 1. Collect insects from the other three subplots. Use an insect field guide to identify the types of insect found in each plot, then record the number of each type found. Take photos of each insect jar, then release the insects where they were collected. Display the photos.

3. Make molds of any animal tracks in each subplot by pouring plaster of paris into the tracks. Mix the plaster of paris by following the directions on the package. Use the molds as part of a project display.

## CHECK IT OUT!

An ecosystem that covers a large geographic area where plants of one type live due to the specific climate in the area is called a *biome*. What are the five basic biomes? For information about biomes, see pages 73–74 in *Janice VanCleave's Ecology for Every Kid* (New York: Wiley, 1996).

# 10 Nibblers

## PROBLEM

*How does grass survive when eaten to the ground by animals?*

## Materials

potting soil
9-ounce (270-ml) paper cup
trowel
clump of grass
pencil
saucer
tap water
ruler
marking pen

## Procedure

1. Put the soil in the cup.
2. With an adult's permission, use the trowel to dig up a clump of grass that will fit in the paper cup. Choose a clump that has at least three grass stems, and make sure you dig up as many of the grass roots as possible.
3. Plant the grass in the soil.
4. Use the pencil to punch three or four holes on the side of the cup around the bottom edge.
5. Set the cup in the saucer.
6. Moisten the soil with water and keep the soil moist, but not wet, during the experiment.
7. Use the diagram to locate each **node** (the joint on a plant stem where a leaf is generally attached) and **internode** (the area between two consecutive nodes) on each grass stem.
8. Use the ruler and pen to mark three equal sections on the stem's first internode (the highest one on the stem).
9. Repeat step 8 for the other two stems, marking the second and third highest pairs of nodes, respectively.
10. Set the plant in an area where it will receive sunlight all or most of the day.
11. At the end of 7 days, measure the distance between the marks on the stems.

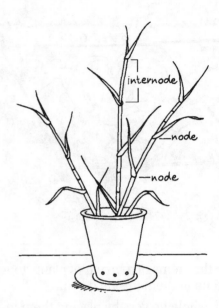

## Results

For each internode, the distance between the lower node and the first mark above this node increases the most on all the stems. Any increase in distance between the remaining marks is slight to none as the marks approach the higher node.

## Why?

Upright grass stems above ground are called **culms** and are made of two parts: nodes and internodes. Nodes are solid joints where leaves are generally attached. The internodes, or areas between the nodes, are usually hollow, but may be **pithy** (soft and spongy) or solid. Generally, stems of dicot plants grow at their tips. But stems of many monocots, such as grasses, grow just above each node along the stem. When an upper section of a grass stem is cut off, the lower part of the stem continues to grow. This type of growth allows grass to survive when nibbled to the ground by various animals.

## LET'S EXPLORE

Is there any difference in the amount of growth in different internodes along the same grass stem or in the internodes of different grass stems? Repeat the experiment, measuring and recording the length of three or more internodes on each of three or more stems. Record the initial and final lengths of the internodes for each internode of all stems in a data chart similar to the one shown. Use the following equation and example to determine the amount of growth for each internode.

growth = final length – starting length
       = 6 inches (15 cm) – 4 inches (10 cm)
       = 2 inches (5 cm)

### GRASS STEM 1

| Internode Number | Starting Length | Final Length | Growth |
|---|---|---|---|
| #1 | 4 inches (10 cm) | 6 inches (15 cm) | 2 inches (5 cm) |

## SHOW TIME!

**1a.** Use the following steps to make a model to show the different grazing animals in the grasslands of east Africa and the different parts of the grass plant that they eat.

- Fold 2 sheets of typing paper in half lengthwise.

- Unfold the papers, then fold them in half widthwise (from top to bottom) twice.

- Unfold one of the papers. On the left side, draw or glue pictures of a zebra, wildebeest, and Thomson's gazelle. The animals must be in the order shown. Write "Tropical Grassland Grass-Eaters" in the bottom left section.

- Unfold the other sheet of paper, then use a ruler and pen to draw a line across the paper along each of the three parallel fold lines. Make the lines dashed on the left side of the lengthwise center fold and solid on the right side of this fold.

- Write "Guide to Grass-Eaters" in the bottom left section, number the three sections above this label, and draw a grass plant on the right side of the center fold as shown.

- Cut along the dashed lines so that each numbered section becomes a flap. On the underside of the flaps, write "Top-Eater," "Middle-Eater," and "Bottom-Eater," starting with flap 1 as "Top-Eater."

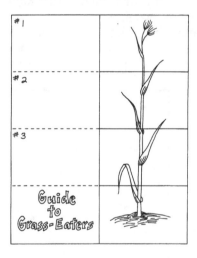

- Lay this sheet over the sheet that has the animal drawings, and secure the papers together with tape along the top, bottom, and side of the right half of the guide.

**b.** In grasslands there are many different kinds of animals grazing on grass. Find out more about animals that feed on grasses. Use your Guide to Grass-Eaters to explain how grazing animals feed on different parts of the grass plant.

# 11 It Takes Two

## PROBLEM

*How does a Punnett square predict possible gene combinations?*

## Materials

marking pen
ruler
typing paper (or any writing paper)

## Procedure

1. Draw a 2-inch (5-cm) square on the paper.

2. Divide the square into four smaller squares by drawing two lines, one vertical and one horizontal, through the center of the square.

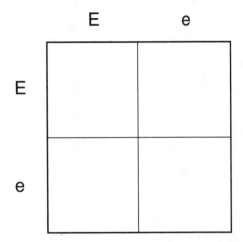

3. Label the squares *E* and *e* across the top and down the left side of the large square as shown.

4. In each small square, write the letters that appear above and to the left of the square, writing capital letter first.

## Results

There are three different combinations of letters in the boxes: *EE, Ee,* and *ee.*

## Why?

The letter combinations stand for combinations of genes. **Genes** (locations on a chromo-

some that determine inherited traits), located in **chromosomes** (threadlike structures in cells that carry instructions, much like a computer program, to make the cell function), determine inherited traits. **Traits** are characteristics, such as hair color, eye color, and height, that help to identify living organisms. For each inherited trait, the offspring has two genes, one from the father and one from the mother. The gene that determines the trait is called the **dominant gene**, represented by a capital letter. The other gene, called a **recessive gene**, is represented by a lowercase letter. If both genes are either dominant or recessive, the trait is called a **pure trait**. If only one gene is dominant, the combination is said to be a **hybrid trait**. Gene combinations are written with the dominant gene (represented by a capital letter) first.

In this activity, you will use a **Punnett square** to show all possible gene combinations that can be transferred from parents to offspring for the trait of earlobe attachment. *E* represents the dominant gene for unattached earlobes, and *e* represents the recessive gene for attached earlobes. Because unattached earlobes are dominant, the combination *EE* is a pure trait for unattached earlobes, while *Ee* is a hybrid for unattached earlobes. Both parents have the hybrid, as shown by the *E* and *e* along both the top and side of the large square. Three of the smaller squares show combinations—*EE, Ee,* and *Ee*—that would give the offspring unattached earlobes. The fourth square shows the combination *ee*, which would give the offspring attached earlobes, a pure trait determined by recessive genes.

## LET'S EXPLORE

What are the possible combinations if one parent has pure trait genes (*EE*) and the other has hybrid genes (*Ee*)? Repeat the activity, using the letters *E* and *E* across the top and *E* and *e* down the side. **Science Fair Hint:** Use the Punnett squares as part of a project display.

## SHOW TIME!

1. Although the Punnett square shows the possible combinations, it cannot be used to predict

## Father

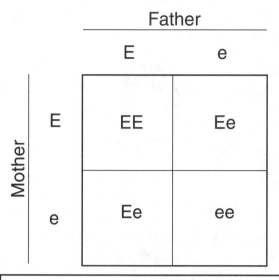

|  | E | e |
|---|---|---|
| **E** | EE | Ee |
| **e** | Ee | ee |

Mother

**Legend**

| Genes | Combinations |
|---|---|
| E  unattached earlobes | EE  pure (unattached earlobes) |
| e  attached earlobes | Ee  hybrid (unattached earlobes) |
| | ee  pure (attached earlobes) |

what will actually happen to each child if four children are born to the same parents. Coins can be used to show how chance affects **heredity** (the passing on of traits from parents to offspring). Place a small piece of tape on the front and back of each of 2 pennies. Write a capital *E* on one side of each penny and a lower case *e* on the other side.

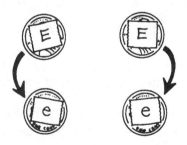

Stretch a small hand towel out on a table. Hold both coins in your hands and shake them back and forth several times, then toss the coins together over the towel. *NOTE: The towel will prevent the coins from rolling off the table.* Prepare a chart as shown to record the letter combinations. Toss the coins three more times, recording each letter combination.

Compare the four combinations to those in the Punnett square of the original experiment.

2. Repeat the previous experiment twice, using different gene combinations for the father and mother. Prepare a chart as before to record the results of each experiment. First use pure trait from dominant genes (*EE*) and hybrid (*Ee*), then use pure trait from recessive genes (*ee*) and hybrid (*Ee*). Prepare a Punnett square for each gene combination. Use the charts and Punnett squares as part of a project display.

3. How are you similar to or different from each of your parents? Examine some of your genetic traits and the genetic traits of your parents. Design and prepare a chart showing the presence or absence of the traits being examined. Possible traits to look for are right- or left-handedness, eye color, dimples, freckles, ear lobes (attached or unattached), and eye shape (round or oval). Use the results to prepare a written and/or oral presentation. Provide proof that you do not receive all of your genes from only one parent.

## CHECK IT OUT!

*Inherited traits* are traits passed from parents to offspring. For more information about heredity, see pages 193–201 of *Janice VanCleave's The Human Body for Every Kid* (New York: Wiley, 1995).

# 12 Boy or Girl

## PROBLEM

*What are the chromosome combinations that produce a boy or a girl?*

### Materials

masking tape
marking pen
2 coffee cups
3 red kidney beans
1 white lima bean
drawing compass
sheet of typing paper

### Procedure

1. Use the tape and marking pen to label one cup Ova and the other cup Sperm.

2. Place 2 red kidney beans in the cup labeled Ova and 1 red kidney bean in the cup labeled Sperm.

3. Add the white lima bean to the sperm cup.

4. Set the cups on a table

5. Use the compass to draw two circles with a 2-inch (5-cm) diameter on the paper.

6. Place the paper on the table near the cups.

7. Without looking into the cups, take 1 bean out of each and place the 2 beans in one of the circles drawn on the paper.

8. Repeat step 7, placing the beans in the other circle.

### Results

Each circle has 2 beans in it. One circle has 2 red beans and one circle has a red and a white bean.

### Why?

The sex of a baby is due to two sets of instructions. These instructions are in the sex chromosomes, known as X and Y. Females have two X chromosomes, and males have an X and a Y. An **ovum** (female sex cell, or egg) and a **sperm** (male sex cell) have one sex chromosome each.

Ova have only X chromosomes, while half of the sperm have X chromosomes and half have Y chromosomes. The joining of an ovum and a sperm is called **fertilization**, and the fertilized egg is called a **zygote**. If an ovum is fertilized by a sperm carrying a Y chromosome, the XY combination produces a boy. If the ovum is fertilized by a sperm carrying an X chromosome, the XX combination produces a girl.

The red beans in this experiment represent X chromosomes and the white bean a Y chromosome. The combination of 2 red beans indicates a girl, and a red-and-white combination a boy. The sex chromosome from the sperm determines the sex of the baby. The combinations of the beans in the experiment represent one boy and one girl.

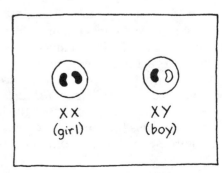

## LET'S EXPLORE

Are the odds of a baby being a boy or a girl always 50-50? If three families each have four children, will each family have two boys and two girls? Repeat the experiment, placing 12 red kidney beans in the ova cup. Since there is usually one egg but many available sperm to combine with it, place 12 red kidney beans and 12 lima beans in the sperm cup. Draw 12 circles on a sheet of poster board as shown in the diagram. Take 1 bean out of each cup and place the pairs in one of the circles. Fill the four circles for the first family, then fill them for the other two families. **Science Fair Hint:** Glue the beans to the poster board and record how many boys (XY) and girls (XX) are in each family. Create a Legend. Use the poster board and Legend as part of a project display.

| Family | Children | B | G |
|--------|----------|---|---|
| 1 | ○ ○ ○ ○ | | |
| 2 | ○ ○ ○ ○ | | |
| 3 | ○ ○ ○ ○ | | |

## SHOW TIME!

Would the chance of having a boy or a girl be 50-50 if more children were born? Use a pen, ruler, and paper to prepare a chart, like the one shown at the bottom of the page, for 15 families.

Stretch a small hand towel out on a table. Hold 6 pennies in your hand and shake them back and forth several times, then toss the coins together over the towel. *NOTE: The towel will prevent the coins from rolling off the table.* Count the number of heads and tails, and write the numbers in the columns for Family 1. Toss the coins 14 more times, recording the results for each family. Use the results to determine whether each of the 15 families shows a **ratio** (a numerical comparison of two different things) of exactly half boys and half girls. Does the total number of girls and boys in all the families show a ratio of 50-50?

## CHECK IT OUT!

Find out more about fertilization in humans. Where does it occur? Where are sperm and ova produced? For information, see pages 185–189 of *Janice VanCleave's The Human Body for Every Kid* (New York: Wiley, 1995).

| PROBABILITY OF HAVING A GIRL OR A BOY | | |
|---|---|---|
| Family | Heads (girls) | Tails (boys) |
| 1 | | |
| 2 | | |
| 3 | | |
| 4 | | |
| ... | | |
| 15 | | |
| Totals | | |

# Floaters

## PROBLEM

*How can you grow the mold penicillium?*

## Materials

baby food jar
dishwashing liquid
warm tap water
apple cider
magnifying lens

## Procedure

*WARNING: After performing the experiments in this chapter, discard all molds and the foods on which they are grown. CHOOSE ANOTHER PROJECT IF YOU ARE ALLERGIC TO MOLD.*

1. Wash the jar with warm, soapy water and rinse with warm water.
2. Fill the jar with apple cider.
3. Place the open jar of apple cider in a warm, dark place.
4. Use the magnifying lens to make daily observations of the surface of the cider for 2 weeks.

## Results

After a few days, growths that look like round, fuzzy, blue-green pads will be floating on the surface of the cider. These growths resemble floating lily pads. In time, the growths will cover the entire surface of the liquid.

## Why?

The fuzzy growth on the surface of the apple cider is the mold **penicillium**. (A **mold** is a fuzzy fungi growth produced on food and damp surfaces.) The time it takes for penicillium to grow depends on the temperature of the room. In a warm room, signs of growth may appear in 2 to 3 days. The blue-green color and fuzzy appearance are caused by the production of **spores** (one-celled bodies that are capable of developing into new organisms). Penicillium is a common fungi. **Fungi** are simple, plantlike organisms that cannot make their own food. Penicillium spores are produced at the top of threadlike parts called **hyphae** (singular **hypha**), which make up the base of the floating pad. The tangled mass of hyphae is called a **mycelium**.

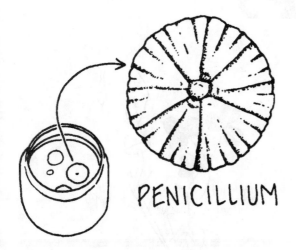

PENICILLIUM

water to the inside of the bag. Seal the bag and place it in a dark, warm place for 10 days. Use a magnifying lens to observe the surface of the bread daily for signs of mold. Make colored diagrams of your observations.

**b.** At the end of 10 days, ask an adult to cut a thin piece from the bread. Place the piece on a microscope slide. Slowly move the slide around as you observe the bread under low power, with the slide brightly lit from above by a desk lamp. Make a colored diagram to display with diagrams of the bread mold observed with the magnifying lens.

## TRY IT WITH A MICROSCOPE
### Microscope Procedure

1. Collect a sample of the mold by brushing an art brush across the surface of the mold.
2. Tap the brush on a clean microscope slide.
3. Observe the slide under low power.
4. Adjust the mirror or light below the slide to produce as much illumination as possible.
5. Move the slide around to view different areas.

### Microscope Results

Dark clumps and specks as well as threadlike structures are seen across the viewing field.

### LET'S EXPLORE

1. Would penicillium grow in a closed jar? Repeat the original experiment, placing a lid on the jar.
2. Does the type of fruit juice affect the results? Repeat the original experiment, using other fruit juices such as cranberry, grape, and cherry.

### SHOW TIME!

**1a.** Grow bread mold by placing a slice of bread in a sealable plastic bag. Add 10 drops of

## CHECK IT OUT!

Penicillium is used to make penicillin. Besides its medicinal purposes, it is used to make cheeses such as Roquefort, also called blue cheese because of the large number of spores present. Find out more about penicillium and other molds. What is an antibiotic? How did the British scientist Sir Alexander Fleming (1881–1955) discover that penicillium had antibiotic properties? What are other helpful uses of molds? How are molds harmful?

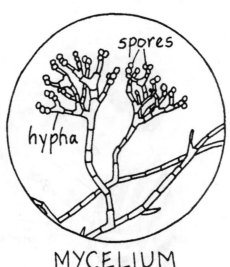

MYCELIUM

# 14

# Bumpy

### PROBLEM

*How do bacteria help clover live?*

### Materials

trowel
clover
1-quart (1-liter) plastic bucket
tap water
2 paper towels
magnifying lens

### Procedure

1. With an adult's permission, use the trowel to dig up a clump of clover. Be sure to get as much of the root as possible.

2. Fill the bucket about halfway with water.

3. Dip the roots of the clover up and down in the bucket of water until the roots are free of dirt.

4. Lay the wet plant on the paper towel. Blot the plant with another paper towel to absorb any excess water.

5. Study the roots of the plant carefully with the magnifying lens. Find the nodules (rounded bumps) growing on the roots.

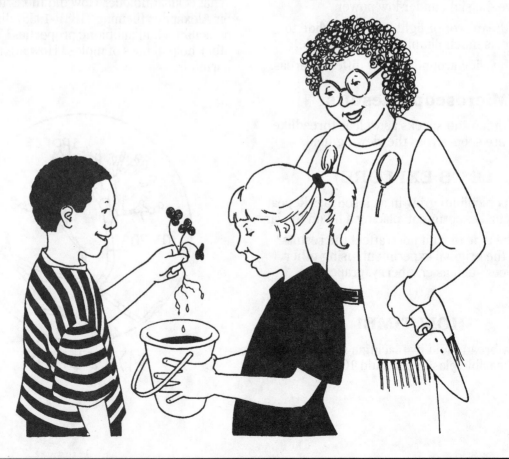

## Results

Small nodules that look like tiny potatoes appear to be growing on the roots. Some of the nodules are separate and appear at different places along the roots; however, most of the nodules are grouped together in clumps at the top of the roots.

## Why?

In order to live, plants need the nitrogen compounds that are found in soil. Nitrogen gas makes up 78 percent of the earth's atmosphere, but plants cannot use this form of nitrogen. Bacteria called **nitrogen-fixing bacteria** change nitrogen gas into nitrogen compounds that plants can use. Some nitrogen-fixing bacteria live in the soil, while others live on the roots of plants such as clover. The bacteria enter the root hairs of the plant, and as they multiply, a nodule forms. The bacteria and clover help each other. The bacteria "fix" nitrogen gas so that the plant can use it, and the plant provides food for the bacteria. This is an example of **symbiosis**, a relationship in which two organisms, living together, are mutually benefited.

## TRY IT WITH A MICROSCOPE

### Microscope Procedure

1. Use scissors to cut a section about ½ inch (1.3 cm) long from one of the smaller roots. The piece must contain at least one small nodule.

2. Place the root section on a microscope slide.

3. Position a desk lamp so that the slide is brightly lit from above.

4. Adjust the mirror or light under the stage of the microscope to produce a dark background for the viewing field.

5. Slowly move the slide around while viewing it under low power.

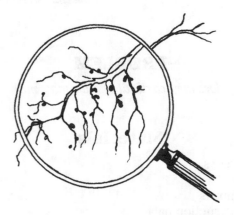

## Microscope Results

The outside surface of the nodules looks rough and bumpy, while the root has a smoother appearance.

## LET'S EXPLORE

1. Are the nodules hollow? Ask an adult to cut a nodule in half. Use a magnifying lens to examine the contents of the nodule.

2. Place the open nodule on a microscope slide and examine it using the previous microscope procedure. **Science Fair Hint:** Use photographs of the clover nodules, along with diagrams of images viewed through the microscope, as part of a project display.

## SHOW TIME!

People are simply imitating nature when they recycle resources. Elements that are important to life, such as nitrogen, are naturally recycled. Nitrogen is found in the air, in soil, and in all living things. Use a biology text to find a diagram of the nitrogen cycle. Prepare a display chart of the nitrogen cycle. Photograph plants and animals needed for the chart, and use the photographs on the chart instead of drawings.

## PROBLEM

*Why does the heartbeat of mammals make a sound?*

## Materials

scissors
glue
compass
construction paper
large thread spool
timer
pencil
transparent tape

## Procedure

1. Cut and glue a circle of construction paper to cover each end of the thread spool. Allow the glue to dry for several hours.

2. Use a pencil to punch a hole in each paper circle to line up with the hole in the spool.

3. Cut a smaller paper circle about 1 inch (2.5 cm) in diameter.

4. Center this small paper circle over the paper circle on one end of the spool, and secure it on one side with a piece of tape about ¼ inch (0.6 cm) wide. This makes a flap over the hole.

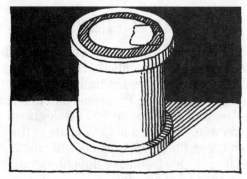

5. With your mouth, blow through the hole in the uncovered end of the spool so that the paper flap on the other end opens out.

6. Suck air back through the hole with enough force to cause the paper flap to close against the end of the spool.

7. Repeat the blowing and sucking of air through the hole in the spool.

8. Listen to the sound made as the paper flap opens and closes.

BLOW OUT

SUCK IN

## Results

A swishing sound is heard when the flap opens out, and a thumping sound each time the flap closes.

## Why?

In all mammals, the heart is a double pump. Each side of the heart has an upper and lower chamber. The top chambers are called **atriums** and the lower chambers are called **ventricles**. A one-way flap called a **valve** (structure that controls blood flow in one direction) connects the upper and lower chambers. When the heart muscle relaxes, blood flows through the open valves from the atriums into the ventricles. When the heart contracts, the flap is closed with a thump. The valve prevents the blood from moving back into the atrium, and it is forced out of the heart through another opening. The opening and closing of the paper flap on the thread spool produces a sound like that made by heart valves. The sound from the valves can be heard through the **tissues** (groups of similar cells that perform special functions) of the body and is often described as a lub-dub sound.

## LET'S EXPLORE

Would a hole in the flap affect the sound? Repeat the experiment, making a small hole in the paper flap. Repeat several times, making increasingly larger holes in the flap.

## SHOW TIME!

1. How can blood flow in only one direction in veins? **Veins** (blood vessels that carry blood to the heart) have valves. Build a model using a box and two flaps of stiff paper to demonstrate the movement of blood through the one-way valves in blood vessels. Use a marble to represent blood. Tape one flap to one of the long sides of the box so that it moves when the marble hits it. This is the movable flap. Tape the other flap to the opposite side of the box. This is the stationary flap. Make sure the stationary flap is wide enough so that the movable flap overlaps it by about ½ inch (1.25 cm). Put the marble in the box and tilt the box forward so that the marble hits the movable flap and opens it. Tilt the container backward, and the marble hits against the flap, closing it. Use your model, along with diagrams of a vein, as part of a project display. Find out how blood flows in **arteries** (blood vessels that carry blood away from the heart).

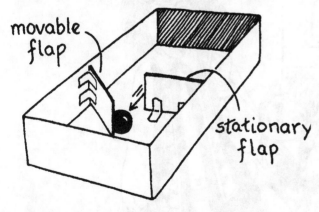

movable flap

stationary flap

2. How much blood moves with each heartbeat? This can vary with the size of the heart. In humans, the average is about ¼ cup (63 ml) per beat, or about 5 quarts (5 liters) per minute. Demonstrate the work done by the heart by using a ¼-cup (63-ml) measuring cup to transfer 5 quarts (5 liters) of water from one container to another. Remember that the job must be done in 1 minute. Dip the measuring cup into the water, and pour the water into the other container. Photographs of this experiment are the best way to display the procedure. Count each transfer to determine the number of times the heart must beat in 1 minute in order to pump 5 quarts (5 liters) of blood.

## CHECK IT OUT!

1. Animals have hearts with two or more chambers that pump blood through their circulatory system. Discover more about the hearts of different animals. How do the hearts of fish, amphibians, mammals, and birds differ? What is the specific difference between the hearts of birds and mammals? Use diagrams of animal hearts as part of your project display.

2. Insect blood is usually greenish in color. Some insects have pulsating sacs in their knee joints that push the blood throughout the body. Find out more about the circulatory system of insects.

# 16 Instant Flies

## PROBLEM

*Can flies grow from decaying bananas?*

## Materials

masking tape
marking pen
two 1-quart (1-liter) jars
banana

## Procedure

*NOTE: This experiment works best during warm weather.*

1. Use the tape and marking pen to label the jars #1 and #2.

2. Peel the banana and place the fruit inside jar #2.

3. Leave the jars open and undisturbed for 2 weeks.

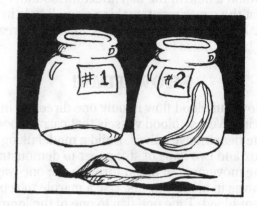

4. Observe and record your observations daily for 14 days, using a chart like the one shown.

## Results

These results were observed:
- Brown spots appeared on the banana.
- The entire banana looked dark brown and moist.

- Flies appeared and were seen inside each jar.
- Maggots appeared in the jar with the rotting fruit but not in the empty jar.

## Why?

A popular theory until the 18th century was that living organisms such as maggots come from dead matter. The theory that living organisms come from nonliving material is called **spontaneous generation theory**. This theory was disproved about 100 years ago, and, through further experimentation, it was proved that gases released by the rotting fruit attract the flies. The flies lay their eggs in the fruit, and the eggs hatch into tiny, white wormlike organisms called maggots. Given enough time, the maggots grow into adult flies. Thus, the maggots observed in the jar with the fruit are just one stage in the life of a fly.

## LET'S EXPLORE

1. Would the maggots appear if the jar with the banana were closed? Repeat the experiment, using 3 jars. Label the third jar #3 and place a peeled banana in it. Seal jar #3 with a lid. Observe and record the results daily.

2. Will the rotting of other fruits result in the appearance of maggots? Repeat the original experiment, replacing the banana with other fruit. Keep daily records of your observations for display.

3. Use the procedure of a famous experiment designed by Francesco Redi (1626–1697) to confirm that decaying food does not produce living organisms. Place small pieces of fruit in 3 separate jars. Leave one jar open, seal one with a lid, and cover the third jar with a cotton handkerchief. **Science Fair Hint:** Keep daily records of your observations for display. Find out more about Redi's experiment and use it in your project report.

## SHOW TIME!

Use biology texts to discover different popular beliefs about spontaneous generation, and represent them with drawings. The recipe here for producing mice was created by a man named Jan van Helmont (1577–1644). Use a drawing similar to the one shown as part of a project display. *CAUTION: Do not try this at home!*

## VAN HELMONT'S RECIPE FOR MICE

### Ingredients

dark container
1 cup (250 ml) wheat grains
dirty shirt

### Directions

1. Put the dirty shirt and the wheat grains together in the container.

2. Wait several days.

Yields many mice.

## CHECK IT OUT!

Antonie van Leeuwenhoek's (1637–1723) discovery of microorganisms made scientists question whether the tiny creatures that appear so quickly in rotting food might arise spontaneously. Discover how an Italian priest named Lazzaro Spallanzani (1729–1799) tried to disprove this. Why was his experiment not respected by other scientists?

# Fatty Insulators

## PROBLEM

*Does the fat layer under the skin keep an animal warm?*

## Materials

two 9-ounce (270-ml) paper cups
shortening
2 bulb-type thermometers
clock

## Procedure

*NOTE: This experiment requires access to a freezer.*

1. Fill one of the paper cups with shortening.

2. Insert one of the thermometers into the cup of shortening so that the bulb of the thermometer is in the center of the shortening.

3. Stand the second thermometer in the second, empty paper cup. *NOTE: Lay the cup on its side if the weight of the thermometer causes the cup to topple over.*

4. Read and record the temperature shown on each thermometer. Then, place the cups with their thermometers in the freezer and shut the door.

5. Read and record the temperature shown on each thermometer every 3 minutes for 30 minutes.

6. Read the thermometers again after 24 hours.

## Results

After 30 minutes, the reading on the thermometer placed in the shortening changed very little, but the temperature inside the empty cup decreased rapidly. After 24 hours, both thermometers read the same.

## Why?

Heat energy moves from a warmer place to a colder place. When heat energy moves away from an object, that object becomes cooler. Its temperature gets lower. **Insulators** are materials that slow down the transfer of heat energy. The shortening, like the fat layer under the skin of animals, acts as an insulator and thus restricts the flow of heat away from the warm inner body to the frigid air outside the body. The heat inside the shortening, like that in the insulating fat in an animal's body, is lost, but the loss is very slow. Given enough time, a great amount of heat can be lost. The shortening cools to air temperature, but food eaten by animals provides energy that continuously replaces the lost heat. Thus, a constant body temperature is maintained.

## LET'S EXPLORE

Are fatter animals warmer? Repeat the experiment, using different amounts of shortening. Use the materials and/or photographs of the experiment along with the results as part of a project display.

## SHOW TIME!

1. A special system of blood vessels exists in the extremities of penguins. This system keeps their less insulated feet and flippers from lowering their body temperature. The arteries carrying warm blood to the feet and flippers are surrounded by veins carrying cold blood away

from the feet and flippers. The cold blood is warmed before it reaches the body, and the warm blood is cooled before reaching the feet. Demonstrate this energy exchange by placing a container of warm water inside a larger container of cold water. Place a thermometer inside each container. Keep a record of the temperature in both containers until no further changes are observed. Display drawings of the containers and a written explanation of the results.

2. Show how color of an animal's feathers or hair affects its body temperature. Black objects absorb more light waves than white objects. This absorption of the waves of energy causes the object's temperature to rise. Cover the bulb of one thermometer with white paper and the bulb of a second thermometer with black paper. Place the thermometers in direct sunlight and keep a record of their temperature readings for about 20 minutes. Use photographs and diagrams along with the results as part of a display.

## CHECK IT OUT!

The male emperor penguin *incubates* (keeps warm and protected in order to hatch) the one egg laid by his mate. This is done by rolling the egg onto his feet and covering it with a special fold of skin on the bottom of his stomach, which has several rolls of fat. Find out more about the nesting habits of different penguin species. How long does the male emperor stand with the egg on his feet? How do the nesting habits of Adélie and emperor penguins differ?

# 18 Reflectors

## PROBLEM

*Do cats' eyes glow in the dark?*

### Materials

scissors
construction paper
empty coffee can (inside bottom must be
   shiny)
masking tape
flashlight

### Procedure

1. Cut a circle from the construction paper large enough to cover the end of the can.
2. In the center of the paper circle, cut a long oval opening.
3. Tape the paper circle over the open end of the can. This is a model of a cat's eye.

4. In a darkened room, hold the can at arm's length and at eye level in front of you so that the opening in the paper faces you.
5. Look toward the opening in the paper, and record your observations.
6. Hold the flashlight in front of your face and shine the light toward the opening in the paper.
7. Again, look toward the opening and record your observations.

### Results

The can is not very visible in the darkened room. When a flashlight is shined toward the can, the shiny bottom of the can and the paper glow.

### Why?

Cats' eyes do not "glow" in the dark. The glow from the animal's eyes is due to the reflection of external light. The back of each cat's eye has mirrorlike cells that, like the bottom of the coffee can, reflect light. These cells are filled with a chemical called **guanine** that reflects even the smallest amounts of light and thus floods the eyeball with light, causing it to appear to glow. The eyes do not appear to glow during the day because the dark, oval-shaped slit in the animal's eyes (called the **pupil**) is only slightly open. Any light reflected during the day is not noticed because of the brightness of the sun's light.

## LET'S EXPLORE

1. At night, a cat's pupil opens exceptionally wide, allowing more light from a flashlight or other external light source to enter and be reflected from the back of the eye. Demonstrate how the size of the pupil relates to the amount of glow of the cat's eye. Repeat the experiment, changing the size of the oval slit in the paper circle. **Science Fair Hint:** Display the paper circles used in order of their ability to produce a glow.

2. Humans and other animals with good day vision have a thin layer of heavily pigmented tissue, called **choroid,** on the back of the eye. Demonstrate how the choroid layer absorbs light. Repeat the experiment, covering the shiny bottom of the can with a piece of black construction paper. Use the materials and the results as part of a project display.

## SHOW TIME!

In dim light or darkness, the muscles in the front of the eye of all animals relax, causing the

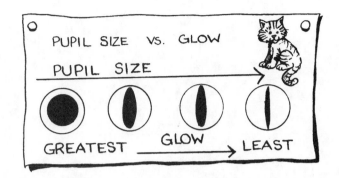

pupil to enlarge. To observe the effect that light has on the size of the pupil, sit in a brightly lit room for 2 minutes. Keep one eye tightly closed and the other eye open. Observe the pupil of the open eye by looking in a mirror. Open the closed eye and immediately observe the size of the pupil. Notice and record the difference in the size of each pupil. Have a helper take photographs of you as you perform this experiment, or make drawings showing the size of your pupils, to use as part of your project display.

## CHECK IT OUT!

Nocturnal hunters (animals that hunt at night) tend to have long, oval-shaped pupils, while daytime prowlers have round pupils. Find out how the shape of the pupil affects an animal's ability to see.

# Earth Science

dishwashing
liquid

paper
plate

clay

Dew Point

Lauren's
sugar

crystal

Gelatin

MIKE

# Easy Flow

## PROBLEM

*How does pressure affect rock in the astheno-sphere?*

## Materials

1-cup (250-ml) measuring cup
tap water
9-oz (270-ml) plastic drinking glass
1-tablespoon (15-ml) measuring spoon
10 tablespoons (150 ml) cornstarch
spoon
bowl

## Procedure

1. Prepare simulated "putty rock" by following these steps:

   • Pour ¼ cup (63 ml) of water into the plastic glass.

   • Add 1 level tablespoon (15 ml) of cornstarch and stir well. Continue adding cornstarch, 1 tablespoon (15 ml) at a time, stirring well after each addition. *NOTE: The mixture should be thick enough that it is very hard to stir.* Add a few drops of water if all of the starch will not dissolve, or add a little starch if the mixture looks thin.

2. Set the bowl on a table.

3. Hold the glass containing the putty rock in one hand, and tilt the glass slightly so that about half of the material flows slowly into the bowl.

4. Observe how the material flows.

5. Use the spoon to scrape the rest of the material out of the glass and into the bowl.

6. Observe how the material behaves when forced to move.

7. Return the putty rock to the glass and keep it for the next experiment.

## Results

The material flows easily out of the glass when allowed to flow freely, but cracks and breaks if forced to move.

## Why?

The earth can be divided into three main sections: core, mantle, and crust. The innermost and hottest section is the **core**. The middle section, called the **mantle**, lies between the core and the thin outer covering, called the **crust**. The crust and the upper portion of the mantle make up a layer that is called the **lithosphere.** Below the lithosphere is a portion of the mantle called the **asthenosphere.** In this zone, the rock making up the mantle behaves like both a liquid and a solid. Rock in the asthenosphere is thought to behave

like the simulated putty rock prepared in the experiment: It flows easily if moved slowly, but thickens and breaks if **pressure** (a force applied over an area) is applied. This ability of a solid material to flow is called **plasticity**.

## LET'S EXPLORE

Would the rate at which the pressure is applied affect the results? Use the prepared simulated putty rock from the original experiment. Apply pressure over a long time period by placing the tip of the spoon against the surface of the putty rock in the glass. Allow the spoon to slide downward slowly. Do not push the spoon. Then, very slowly lift the spoon out of the material. Repeat the action, this time lifting the spoon out very quickly. Notice the difference in response when the pressure is applied slowly or quickly to the material.

## SHOW TIME!

The rift valley through the center of the Mid-Atlantic Ridge, an underwater mountain chain, is growing larger. A **rift valley** is a crack in a ridge that extends into the earth's mantle. In a rift valley there is decreased pressure on the **magma** (molten rock beneath the surface of the earth).

With less pressure, the magma flows more easily and moves upward through the crack. The rising magma cools at the surface, forming a new crustal layer on both sides of the crack. The addition of new material causes the ocean floor surrounding the Mid-Atlantic Ridge to widen by about 1 inch (2.5 cm) per year. As the ocean widens, the continents of Europe and North America move apart.

Yet, the earth is not expanding like an inflated balloon. There are places on the crust that are sinking down into the mantle, allowing the earth's size to remain constant. Demonstrate the rise of magma and the sinking of the crust by asking an adult to help you build two models of a conveyor belt. Follow these steps for each model:

- Place a thread spool at each end of the long, narrow side of a 2-by-4-by-6-inch (5-by-10-by-15-cm) wooden board as shown.
- Insert a nail through the hole of each spool, and hammer the nails into the board. Leave enough space between the spools and the head of the nails so that the spools turn easily.
- Wrap a strip of paper around the spools and tape the ends of the strip together.
- Use a pencil to mark a starting line across the strip.

Turn the two models on their sides, end to end, so that the spools face you. Move each paper strip as needed to bring the starting lines directly opposite each other between the two inner spools. Using your fingers, move the lower part of the paper strips toward the center so that the lines on the paper strips move up and over the inner spools. This action causes the lines to move apart, representing the separation of the ocean floor as magma rises. To represent the sinking of the crust into the earth, move one paper strip in the opposite direction, holding the other stationary.

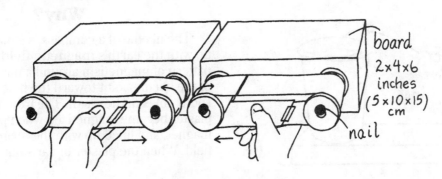

# Mapping

## PROBLEM

*How is the needle of a compass affected by magnetic fields?*

## Materials

craft stick
4 teaspoons (20 ml) plaster of paris
2 teaspoons (10 ml) tap water
paper cup
½ teaspoon (2.5 ml) iron filings (available in a hobby shop)
bar magnet
sheet of paper
compass
marking pen
ruler

*NOTE: Mix the plaster in a throwaway container. Do not wash the container or the craft stick in the sink, because the plaster can clog the drain.*

## Procedure

1. Use the craft stick to mix the plaster of paris and the water in the paper cup.

2. Pour the iron filings into the plaster mixture. Stir well.

3. Set the paper cup on top of the north-pole end of the magnet.

4. Allow the plaster to harden (about 15 to 20 minutes). Then remove the magnet.

5. Place the sheet of paper on a *wooden* table.

6. Turn the cup upside down on top of the paper. Keep the magnet and any magnetic materials away from the cup.

7. Place the compass on the cup's upturned bottom.

8. Starting with the tip of the marking pen about 1 inch (2.5 cm) above the rim of the cup, draw a thick line on the cup that extends onto the paper about 1 inch (2.5 cm) from the cup.

9. Making sure the line on the cup is aligned with the one on the paper, rotate the cup one quarter turn to the right.

10. Wait until the compass needle stops moving, then note the direction that the compass needle is pointing.

11. Continue to turn the cup, one quarter turn at a time, and note the direction of the compass needle. Do this until a complete rotation has been made and the lines are again aligned.

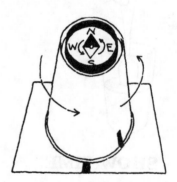

## Results

The needle on the compass points in a different direction after each quarter turn of the cup.

## Why?

The needle of a compass is a magnet that lines up with the earth's **magnetic field** (an invisible pattern of magnetism around a magnet). The ends of the needle point toward the magnetic north and south poles of the earth. The iron filings in the plaster became magnetized when placed near the magnet, and lined up with the magnet's magnetic field. When the plaster of paris hardened, the tiny

plaster with iron filings

iron particles were locked in place, causing the hardened plaster to act like a magnet with magnetic north and south poles. Rotating the cup rotated the "poles" of the iron particles. As a result, the compass needle rotated to line up with the magnetic field of the iron particles, instead of with the magnetic field of the earth.

The earth's magnetic field is currently pointing in a different direction than in times past. Evidence for this shift is found in magnetic rock. It is believed that grains of magnetic material in rock formed from magma and that melted rock lined up with the earth's magnetic field. When the liquid cooled and became a solid, the magnetic grains were locked in place, creating a "map" that pointed in the direction of the earth's magnetic poles. This magnetic map indicates that the magnetic poles of the earth have moved to different places over time.

## LET'S EXPLORE

1. Would it affect the results if the cup were placed on the south pole of the magnet? Repeat the experiment, placing the cup over the south pole of the magnet.

2. Would larger particles of magnetic materials line up with the magnetic field of the magnet and produce the same results as the iron filings? Repeat the original experiment, but substitute steel BBs for the iron filings. **Science Fair Hint:** Display the cups of plaster containing iron filings and BBs, along with a compass

that can be used to demonstrate any change in polarity as the cups are rotated.

## SHOW TIME!

You can make a model of the earth that shows the position of the magnetic and geographic poles. Ask an adult to push a plastic or aluminum knitting needle completely through a Styrofoam ball, as in the diagram. Magnetize a long steel nail so that the head becomes the north pole. Do this by laying the nail on a bar magnet so that the head of the nail is at the north pole of the magnet. Ask an adult to insert the nail completely through the ball at a slight angle to the knitting needle. Tilt the sphere and push the tip of the needle into a lump of modeling clay so that the head of the needle points up at an angle. Label the magnetic and geographic poles on the sphere. Use a compass to demonstrate that the nail attracts the compass needle but the knitting needle does not.

## CHECK IT OUT!

Where are the earth's magnetic north and south poles? Read about the magnetic poles and draw a map showing the present location of the earth's geographic and magnetic poles. It is believed that the poles reverse themselves on the average of once every 1 million years. What causes this change? Draw and display a map showing the wandering of the magnetic poles over millions of years.

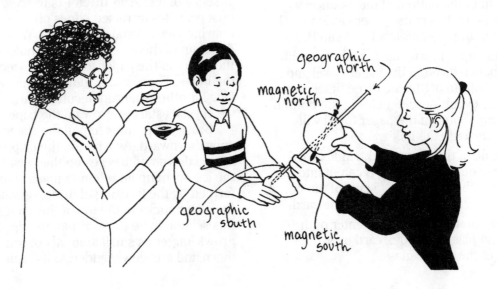

# Icy

## PROBLEM

*How do icicles form?*

## Materials

dressmaker's pin
7-ounce (210-ml) paper cup
marking pen
masking tape
tap water
scissors
paper towel
5-ounce (150-ml) paper cup
sharpened pencil
index card
7-ounce (210-ml) clear plastic glass
timer
adult helper

## Procedure

*NOTE: This experiment requires access to a freezer.*

1. Ask an adult to use the pin to make a pinhole in the center of the bottom of the 7-ounce (210-ml) paper cup. Label this cup A.

2. Cover the hole on the bottom of the cup with a piece of tape.

3. Fill the cup three-fourths full with water.

4. Place the cup in the freezer for 30 minutes.

5. Cut a circle from the paper towel the right size to fit in the bottom of the 5-ounce (150-ml) cup. Insert the paper circle into the bottom of the cup and label this cup B.

6. Holding cup B in one hand, push the point of the pencil through the paper towel and out the bottom of the cup three times to create three evenly spaced holes in the bottom of the cup. Some of the paper towel will extend through the holes.

7. Cut a hole in the center of the index card just large enough that cup B can fit into the hole with about 2 inches (5 cm) of the bottom of the cup extending below the card.

8. Set cup B in the hole in the center of the card, and place the index card over the mouth of the plastic glass.

9. After 30 minutes, remove cup A from the freezer. The water inside cup A should be in liquid form except for a few ice crystals.

10. Remove the tape from the bottom of cup A and place cup A inside cup B.

11. Place the stack of cups in the freezer for 1 hour.

12. Remove the stack of cups and observe.

## Results

A hanging mass of ice extends from each of the three holes in cup B.

## Why?

The water in cup A is below its **freezing point** (the temperature at which a liquid changes to a solid), which for water is 32 degrees Fahrenheit (0°C). This **subcooled water** (liquid water below the freezing point) is cold enough to freeze, but at this temperature, ice crystals will not form in the absence of **freezing nuclei** (surfaces, such as dust particles or raised edges on rough surfaces, on which ice crystals can build). When the water drips out of the cup, some of its molecules stick to the fibers in the paper towel that extend through the holes. These water molecules provide a surface for other water molecules to attach to. Thus, ice crystals start to grow on the paper.

Gravity continues to pull the water drops in the cups downward. As a result, the dripping water moves down and freezes on the outside surface of the ice, forming an **icicle** (a mass of hanging ice formed by the freezing of dripping water). Most of the water sticks to the top of the icicle, causing this section to be thicker than the tip. The icicle grows longer as small amounts of water slide down and are slowly added to its entire length.

## LET'S EXPLORE

1. How much do the hanging fibers in cup B affect the results? Repeat the experiment, but cover only half of cup B with a piece of paper towel. Use the pencil to make two holes through the paper towel and the cup as before. In the side of the cup not covered by the paper towel, make two holes by inserting the pencil point up through the bottom of the cup. **Science Fair Hint:** Display drawings of the results.

2. Do the sizes of the holes in cup B affect the results? Repeat the original experiment, making holes of different sizes in the bottom of cup B.

3. Does the speed of the dripping water affect the results? Repeat the original experiment, using the point of the pencil to make the hole in cup A larger.

## SHOW TIME!

**1a.** Wind plays an important role in the melting of snow, ice, and icicles. Demonstrate this by placing 2 ice cubes of equal size in separate saucers. Place one saucer near a fan set on medium speed, and place the second saucer away from any air movement. Observe the ice cubes to determine which melts faster.

**b.** Determine the effect of wind speed on the melting of ice by repeating the previous experiment twice, first setting the fan on low speed, then setting the fan on high speed. Record and compare the melting time of the ice cubes at each wind speed. Prepare a bar graph to display the results.

2. The six-sided shape of snowflakes is due to the six-sided organization that water molecules assume when they freeze. Make a paper snowflake by drawing a circle on a sheet of plain white paper. Cut out the circle and fold it in half. Fold the half in thirds, like slices of pie, then fold the wedge in half. Cut a small piece out of one curved corner, then cut notches in all the edges, as shown.

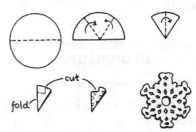

Unfold the paper and you have a six-sided snowflake. This flake can be hung with thread. Make snowflakes of different sizes by changing the size of the original circle. Use the paper snowflakes as part of your project display.

## CHECK IT OUT!

Find out more about snow, ice, and other forms of frozen precipitation. What is sleet? What is freezing rain? How do graupel and ice pellets form? What is the difference between rime and glaze?

# Dew Drops

## PROBLEM

*What causes dew?*

## Materials

2 plastic drinking glasses
tap water
ice
paper towel
timer

## Procedure

1. Fill one of the glasses with water.
2. Fill the second glass with ice, then add enough water to cover the ice.
3. Dry the outside of each glass with the paper towel.
4. Allow the glasses to sit undisturbed for 15 minutes in a draft-free area.
5. Observe the outside of each glass.

## Results

The outside of the glass of water without ice remains dry, but the outside of the glass of ice water is covered with water drops.

## Why?

When air is completely full of water vapor, it is said to be **saturated**. Air may be saturated by adding water vapor, but since less water vapor is needed to saturate cold air, air may become saturated by cooling it. When air is saturated, **condensation** (the change of a gas into a liquid due to a removal of heat energy) occurs.

The ice water cools the glass and the cold glass cools the air around it. Water vapor molecules in this chilled, saturated air clump together, forming tiny drops of visible water. These droplets cling to the outside of the glass and grow as more water condenses on the glass. The glass containing water without ice does not cool the air enough for it to become saturated, so the vapor in the air does not condense. When water vapor in the air comes in contact with cool surfaces, it condenses and forms water droplets called **dew**.

## LET'S EXPLORE

1. Repeat the experiment, using containers made of different materials, such as glass, paper, and metal.

2a. The temperature at which dew forms is called the **dew point**. Determine the temperature at which the dew formed on the glass. Repeat the original experiment, using only the glass of ice water. Place a thermometer in the glass and watch the outside of the glass. Record the temperature when you first observe dew on the outside of the glass.

b. Does **humidity** (the amount of water vapor in the air) affect the dew point? Repeat the previous experiment on different days of varying humidity. Find out the humidity from the local weather reports in the newspaper or on television, and record it for each day the experiment is performed.

## SHOW TIME!

1. Another way of testing how humidity affects dew point is to create a moist environment. Ask an adult to cut the bottom from a 2–liter soda bottle. Secure the cap on the bottle, and set the bottle in a saucer filled with water. Be sure the entire bottom edge of the bottle is below the water in the saucer. Allow the bottle to remain undisturbed overnight. The next day, lift the bottle and place a glass of ice water containing a thermometer in the saucer. Cover the glass with the bottle and observe the out-

side of the glass. Record the temperature at which the dew forms as in the previous experiments.

2. Determine changes in humidity by constructing an instrument used to measure humidity, called a **hygrometer**. Ask an adult to clean the oil from a 6-inch (15-cm) strand of straight hair. If you or your family members do not have straight hair, ask a friend or beautician for a strand. The adult can clean the hair strand by pulling it through 2 cotton balls moistened with nail polish remover.

Use a small piece of tape to secure one end of the strand of hair to the center of a toothpick. Mark the pointed end of the toothpick with a marking pen. Tape the free end of the hair strand to the center of a pencil. Place the pencil across the mouth of a 1-quart (1-liter) jar so that the toothpick hangs inside the jar. If the toothpick does not hang horizontally, add a drop of glue to one end to balance the toothpick. Place the jar where it will not be disturbed. For 1 week or more, make daily observations of the direction in which the toothpick points.

In moist air, the hair lengthens, and in dry air, it shrinks. The stretching and shrinking of the hair pulls on the toothpick and causes it to move. From your results, determine how this hygrometer can be used to measure humidity. Repeat Let's Explore 2a and 2b to determine the effect of humidity on dew point, using your hygrometer to measure humidity.

### CHECK IT OUT!

Dew does not fall from the sky like rain but forms on cool surfaces. Find out more about dew. Why does dew usually form at night? How does the difference between daytime and nighttime temperatures affect the formation of dew?

# Sun Dried

## PROBLEM

*How can the sun be used to separate salt from salt water?*

### Materials

cookie sheet
2 sheets of black construction paper
2 tablespoons (30 ml) table salt
1 cup (250 ml) tap water
spoon

### Procedure

1. Cover the bottom of the cookie sheet with the black paper.

2. Add the salt to the water in the cup and stir. Most, but usually not all, of the salt will dissolve.

3. Pour the salt water over the paper. Try not to pour any undissolved salt onto the paper. Allow the undissolved salt to remain in the cup.

4. Place the cookie sheet in a sunny place where it will not be disturbed for several days. This can be by a window or outdoors if the weather is warm and dry.

5. Observe the paper daily until it is dry.

### Results

At first, a thin layer of white crystals forms on the paper. Later, a few small, separate, white, cubic crystals form.

### Why?

As the sun heats the salt water, the water evaporates and dry salt is left on the paper. While this experiment is similar to a method used by some salt companies to produce salt by the evaporation of seawater, the amount of salt in seawater is much less. This method of salt production is known as the **solar process**, and the product is called **solar salt**. Solar salt is still produced in large amounts in many countries, including the United States.

### LET'S EXPLORE

1. How much solar salt would be produced if the water from a cupful of ocean water evaporated? Repeat the experiment, preparing mock ocean water using 1 teaspoon (5 ml) of salt in the cup of water.

2. A **saltern** is a place where salt is produced by the solar process. A simple saltern can be made by digging a shallow pool near the sea and allowing seawater to flow in. The flow from the sea is then shut off to allow the sun to evaporate the water, leaving a deposit of salt crystals. How does evaporating water from a

shallow pool of salt water affect the salt crystals produced? Repeat the original experiment, replacing the cookie sheet with a small bowl. **Science Fair Hint:** Take photographs of the salt left in this experiment and the original experiment to represent the results. Use the photos as part of a display.

## SHOW TIME!

**1a.** **Salinity** is the measure of the amount of salt dissolved in water. The average salinity of seawater is 35 parts per thousand. This is written as 35 ppt. This means that 35 units of salt are in every 1,000 units of seawater. The gram is the unit most commonly used in measuring salinity, but any unit of **mass** (the amount of material in an object) or **weight** (the force with which an object is pulled toward the center of the earth due to gravity and mass), such as pounds, can be used. While most samples of seawater have a salinity of 35 ppt, it does vary from place to place. The range of salinity of seawater is usually between 32 ppt and 38 ppt. Find out where these salinities are most common, and display a map indicating their location.

**b.** Along with the map, prepare and display photos of samples of the three salinities: 32 ppt, 35 ppt, and 38 ppt. Label the samples and indicate the amount of salt and water in each. Following the example given for the preparation of a sample of seawater with 36 ppt, prepare your three samples.

## Example

*Think!*

- 36 ppt = 36 g salt + 1,000 g water
- Fact: 1 g of water has a volume of 1 ml, thus 1,000 g of water has a volume of 1,000 ml (1 liter).

*Procedure*

1. Fill a jar with 1-liter of water.
2. Use a food scale to measure 36 g of table salt.
3. Add the salt to the water and stir.
4. Label the jar as follows: 36 ppt (36 g salt + 1 liter water).

**2.** Demonstrate the effect that rivers have on ocean salinity by pouring 2 quarts (2 liters) of water into a paint-roller pan. Add 2 tablespoons (30 ml) of table salt and stir. Line the bottom of 4 small bowls with black paper. Use a sharpened pencil to punch a hole in the side and near the bottom of a 3-ounce (90-ml) paper cup. Hold your finger over the hole as you fill the cup half full with water. Add a small pinch of salt to the water to represent the salt in river water. Set the cup on the shallow end of the pan so that the hole points toward the water. Allow the water to flow out of the cup. Quickly take samples of the water from the four places indicated in the diagram (points A, B, C, and D). Use a method of collecting samples, such as a spoon or eyedropper, to ensure that all are the same amount. Place each sample in one of the lined bowls. Place the bowls in a place where the sun can evaporate the water. Then, compare the amount of solar salt left on the paper to determine the effect of the salinity of river water on ocean salinity.

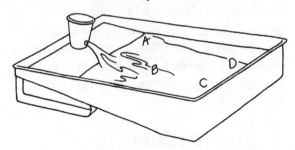

## CHECK IT OUT!

Sodium chloride is the chemical name for the salt known as table salt. This salt is the most abundant salt in seawater. Find out more about sea salts. What are the names of the seven common sea salts and the percentage of each that is found in seawater? What are the uses of these salts? For information, see earth science texts and pages 121–123 in *Janice VanCleave's Oceans for Every Kid* (New York: Wiley, 1996).

## PROBLEM

*How does depth affect the pressure of water?*

## Materials

sharpened pencil
9-ounce (270-ml) paper cup
masking tape
2-quart (2-liter) pitcher
tap water
adult helper

## Procedure

1. Ask an adult to use the pencil to punch two holes of similar diameter in one side of the cup. Make one hole 3 inches (7.5 cm) from the bottom of the cup and the other hole 1 inch (2.5 cm) from the cup's bottom and slightly to the left or right of the top hole.

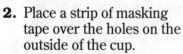

2. Place a strip of masking tape over the holes on the outside of the cup.

3. Fill the pitcher and cup with water.

4. Set the cup on the edge of a sink.

5. Remove the tape from the cup, and ask your helper to keep the cup filled by pouring water from the pitcher into the cup.

6. Observe the distance each stream of water squirts.

## Results

Streams of water squirt out the holes in the cup. The bottom stream squirts farther.

## Why?

Pressure is a force applied over an area. Since water has weight, it exerts pressure. One factor that affects the amount of pressure exerted by water is its depth. The pressure of water increases with depth because of the weight of the water pushing down from above. The greater the pressure, the farther the stream of water squirts, so the stream of water coming from the bottom hole squirts farther.

## LET'S EXPLORE

1. Does pressure increase equally with water depth? Repeat the experiment three times, but make only one hole in the cup at a time. First, experiment with only the top hole. Second, use only the bottom hole. Then, make a hole 2 inches (4 cm) from the bottom of the cup. Design a method to measure the distance that each stream squirts, such as placing a sheet of paper under the streams and marking where they land with a ballpoint pen. Compare the distance between the top and middle streams with the distance between the middle and bottom streams to determine whether pressure increases equally with water depth.

2. Does the amount of water affect its pressure? Repeat the previous experiment, using a larger cup. **Science Fair Hint:** Use diagrams showing the distances between the streams in

the small and large cups as part of a project display.

## SHOW TIME!

The second factor that determines water pressure is its density. **Density** is the "heaviness" of an object, based on its mass compared to its **volume** (the amount of space the object occupies based on its length, width, and depth). As the density of water increases, the pressure that it exerts also increases. How could the density of ocean and fresh water be compared? To find out, use 3 jars with the same mass that are large enough to hold 1 liter of water. Measure the jars to make sure the mass is the same for all three. Since you will need a sensitive scale for these measurements, ask a local pharmacist to assist you in measuring each jar in grams. Prepare the jars as follows:

- Jar 1: Leave empty. Secure lid.
- Jar 2: Fill with 1 liter (1,000 ml) of tap water. Secure lid.
- Jar 3: Fill with 1 liter (1,000 ml) of tap water, add 1 tablespoon (15 ml) of table salt, and stir. Secure lid.

Fill in a data table similar to the one shown here. Use the mass and volume of each jar of water and the density equation shown to determine the density of the fresh and salt water.

*NOTE: The addition of the salt changes the volume of liquid so little that 1,000 ml will be used as the volume of the salt water.*

density = mass of water ÷ 1,000 ml

*NOTE: The density of water is measured in grams per milliliter (g/ml).*

### FRESH AND SALT WATER

| Jar | Material | Mass |
|-----|----------|------|
| 1 | jar + lid | |
| 2 | 1,000 ml fresh water + jar + lid | |
| 3 | 1,000 ml salt water + jar + lid | |

## Example

| Jar | Mass |
|-----|------|
| 1 | 33 g |
| 2 | 1,033 g |

1. Subtract the mass of jar 1 from that of jar 2 to determine the mass of 1,000 ml of fresh water.

| jar 2 (1,000 ml fresh water + jar + lid) | 1,033 g |
|---|---|
| – jar 1 (jar + lid) | 33 g |
| 1,000 ml fresh water | 1,000 g |

2. Use the mass and volume of the fresh water in the density equation:

$$\text{mass} = 1,000 \text{ g}$$
$$\text{volume} = 1,000 \text{ ml}$$
$$\text{density of fresh water} = 1,000 \text{ g} \div 1,000 \text{ ml}$$
$$= 1 \text{ g/ml}$$

## CHECK IT OUT!

Because pressure increases with depth, divers experience physical changes as they descend, or go deeper. At a depth of about 10 feet (3 m), the diver's ears "pop." Find out more about the effects of pressure on a diver. What are the "bends"? How does pressure affect a diver's eyes? What equipment and methods do divers use to protect their bodies? For information, see pages 113–115 in *Janice VanCleave's Oceans for Every Kid* (New York: Wiley, 1996).

# 25 Warm Up

## PROBLEM

*How did the environment affect the body temperature of cold-blooded dinosaurs?*

### Materials

large unruled index card
pencil
one-hole paper punch
scissors
bulb-type thermometer
timer

### Procedure

1. Fold the index card in half lengthwise and open it again. For fun, draw a dinosaur on one side of the folded card.

2. Use the paper punch to make two holes about 1 inch (2.5 cm) apart in the center of the other side of the card.

3. Cut two slits in the paper slightly longer than the width of the thermometer, as shown. Do this by inserting the scissors in each hole and cutting a slit on both sides of the hole.

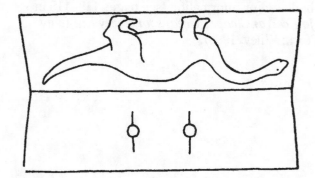

4. Insert the thermometer through the slits in the card so that the bulb is at the tail end of the dinosaur.

5. Read and record the temperature.

6. Stand the dinosaur card outdoors so that the thermometer is in direct sunlight.

7. After 5 minutes, read and record the temperature again.

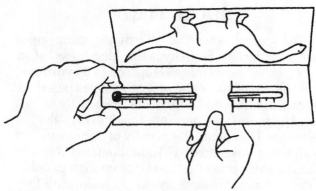

### Results

The temperature reading increases when the card is placed in direct sunlight.

### Why?

**Ectothermic** (cold-blooded) dinosaurs, like ectothermic reptiles of today, were able to increase their body temperature by moving into the sun. The higher temperature reading when the thermometer was placed in the sun indicates that a dinosaur's skin would have received more heat when the animal stood in a sunny area. The blood in the vessels beneath the skin would have warmed, raising the body temperature of the animal.

### LET'S EXPLORE

How could ectothermic dinosaurs cool off? Repeat the experiment twice. First, turn the card so that the head of the dinosaur points directly toward the sun and the thermometer bulb points away from the sun. Then, place the card in a shady area. **Science Fair Hint:** Take photographs of the card in each position. Prepare a chart using the photos and the temperature in each area. Use the chart as part of a project display.

### SHOW TIME!

1. How did dinosaurs keep warm after sunset? Lying against warm soil may have helped dinosaurs stay warm at night. Determine whether soil, after sunset, cools at a slower rate than does the air above it. Do this by measuring the temperature changes of soil and air in a

cold environment. Fill two 12-ounce (360-ml) plastic cups half full with soil. Insert the bulb of a thermometer about ¼ inch (0.63 cm) beneath the soil in one cup. Stand a second thermometer on the surface of the soil in the second cup. Place both cups side by side in a sunny spot. After 5 minutes, read and record the temperature on both thermometers. Keeping the thermometers in the same position, place the cups in a freezer. After 5 minutes, remove the cups from the freezer and again read and record the temperature on both thermometers.

2. Some ectothermic dinosaurs may have had special physical features that helped them control their body heat. For example, the fossil remains of *Spinosaurus* show that this animal had long spines of bone projecting upward from the backbone. These spines are thought to have supported a web of skin like a sail. During the cooler part of the day, *Spinosaurus* could stand with its side to the sun and the blood in the "sail" would heat up like a solar collector. The sun-warmed blood would then carry heat through the animal's body. If the animal became too hot, it could turn the sail away from the sun or move into the shade. Make diagrams or models showing the use of this skin and use them as part of a display.

## CHECK IT OUT!

Find out more about the special physical features used to control the body temperature of some dinosaurs. Some scientists think the plates on the back of *Stegosaurus* may have been used for heat control, not for protection. For more information about these plates and other physical features dinosaurs used for heating and cooling, see pages 117–119 in *Dinosaur!* by David Norman (New York: Prentice Hall General Reference, 1991).

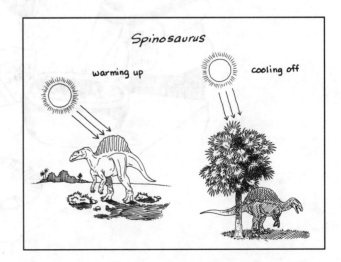

# Imprints

## PROBLEM

*How were dinosaur tracks made?*

## Materials

½ cup (125 ml) flour
½ cup (125 ml) cornmeal
large mixing bowl
spoon
½ cup (125 ml) water
paper plate
8-inch (20-cm)-square baking pan with water

## Procedure

1. Pour the flour and the cornmeal into the bowl and mix with the spoon.

2. Slowly add the water to the flour and cornmeal. Stir until all the water is mixed in. This is your "homemade mud."

3. Pour the mud onto the paper plate. Use the spoon to spread the mud evenly over the plate.

4. Wet one of your hands with water from the pan.

5. Spread the fingers of the wet hand and press the palm side of that hand into the mud.

6. Remove your hand. You should see a good print of your hand. If you do not, do it again.

7. Place the plate on a flat surface where it will not be disturbed, and allow the mud to dry. This may take 2 to 5 days, depending on the temperature and humidity of the air.

## Results

The mud dries, leaving a hard print of the shape of your hand.

## Why?

The soft, homemade mud moved out of the way as you pressed your hand into it. The same thing happens to soft mud when an animal walks or crawls over it. If the **imprint** (marks made by

pressing) made in the soft mud is not disturbed before it dries, a hard print of the animal's tracks forms. Dinosaur tracks have been found in the Connecticut River Valley; GlenRose, Texas; and other places where these prehistoric animals walked in soft mud or sand. In time, the imprints hardened into rock, and the track was trapped forever.

## LET'S EXPLORE

1. Would the amount of water affect the imprint? Make different imprints by using different amounts of water. Keep a record of the amount of water used with each mud mixture. Take photographs of the imprints before and after drying and use the photographs and imprints as part of a project display.

2. Would the type of soil affect the print? Prepare different homemade mud samples by using different amounts of cornmeal and flour. Repeat the experiment twice, first adding more cornmeal, then adding less cornmeal. Make the thickness of the mud in all samples as alike as possible. **Science Fair Hint:** Display imprints along with the recipe of each mixture and a summary stating which sample produced the best imprint.

## SHOW TIME!

How can tracks be collected and studied? You can make plaster of paris (available at art supply stores) and pour it into animal tracks that you find in soil. *NOTE: Mix the plaster in a throwaway container, using a craft stick. Do not wash the container or the craft stick in the sink, because the plaster can clog the drain.* Wait about 20 minutes for the plaster to dry. Then carefully lift the plaster from the soil. You should have a model of the animal's footprint. Present your ideas on what animals made the tracks and give your evidence why.

## CHECK IT OUT!

Discover more about animal tracks and how to identify them. Find a book that shows tracks made by different animals.

# Recorder

## PROBLEM

*How does a seismograph record the magnitude of an earthquake?*

## Materials

cardboard box, measuring about 12 inches (30 cm) on each side
scissors
ruler
adding-machine paper
string
sharpened pencil
5-oz (150-ml) paper cup
masking tape
black marking pen
5 ounces (150 ml) small rocks
modeling clay
adult helper

## Procedure

1.  Ask an adult to prepare the box as follows:

    • Cut the lid off the box, then turn the box on its side so that the opening faces outward.

    • Cut a 2-inch (5-cm)-diameter hole in the center of the top of the box.

    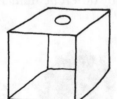

    • Cut two ½-by-4-inch (1.25-by-10-cm) slits in the box. Make the first slit in the center of the bottom, near the opening. Make the second slit, in line with the first slit, in the back of the box.

2.  Cut a 24-inch (60-cm) section of adding-machine paper.

3.  Thread the strip of paper through the slits in the box so that

    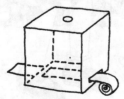

about 2 inches (5 cm) of paper extends past the front edge of the box.

4.  Cut two 18-inch (45-cm) pieces of string.

5.  Ask an adult to use the point of the pencil to punch two opposite holes below the rim of the cup.

6.  Attach the two pieces of string to the cup. Do this by inserting one end of a string through one of the holes, then looping the string over the rim and tying it to itself. Tie the other string to the other hole in the same way.

7.  Set the cup in the box and insert the free end of each string through the hole in the top of the box.

8.  Lay the pencil across the hole and tape the ends of the strings together to the center of the pencil. The bottom of the cup should be about 1 inch (2.5 cm) above the floor of the box.

9.  Push the tip of the marking pen through the inside bottom of the cup.

10. Fill the cup with small rocks to surround the pen.

11. Wind the string around the pencil until the tip of the pen barely touches the adding-machine paper.

12. To prevent the string from unwinding, secure the pencil to the box with a small piece of modeling clay near each end of the pencil.

13. Pull the adding-machine paper toward you with one hand as you gently shake the box with your other hand.

14. Observe the markings made by the pen on the paper.

## Results

The pen draws a zigzag line on the paper as the paper moves underneath the pen.

## Why?

The **inertia** (resistance to a change in motion) of the heavy cup keeps it steady while the box

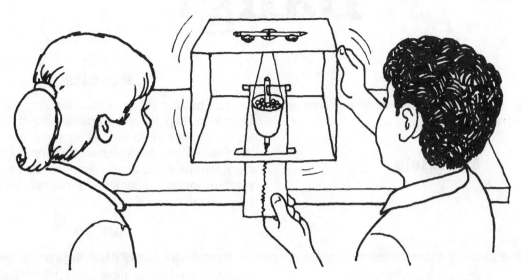

**vibrates** (shakes back and forth repeatedly). As the box vibrates, it moves the paper from side to side underneath the pen; thus, a zigzag line is drawn as the paper is pulled. The shaking energy for an **earthquake** (a violent shaking of the earth's crust caused by a sudden movement of rock beneath its surface) is measured and recorded by an instrument called a **seismograph**. Like your model, a seismograph uses a very heavy suspended object that remains steady, while the frame to which it is attached moves when the earth vibrates. A recording pen attached to the suspended object records the vibrations on the moving paper. The width of the zigzag produced increases with the **magnitude** (measurement of the amount of shaking energy released) of the earthquake being recorded. The written record is called a **seismogram**.

## LET'S EXPLORE

1. Does the weight of the cup affect the seismogram produced? Repeat the experiment, using an empty cup.

2. Does the direction of the earthquake affect the pattern on the seismogram? Use a compass to position the box so that the tape points in a north-to-south direction. Repeat the experiment, shaking the box from the four different directions: north (back), south (front), east (right side), and west (left side). **Science Fair Hint:** Use the model as part of a project display. Label each seismogram with the direction of the vibrations.

## SHOW TIME!

Construct a sensitive seismograph using a beam of light. Place a bowl full of water on a table. Ask a helper to hold a flashlight so that its beam of light falls on the surface of the water and is reflected to a nearby wall. Watch the spot of light on the wall while you gently tap the surface of the water with your finger. Produce other small quakes by tapping the bowl or the table.

## CHECK IT OUT!

Andrija Mohorovicic (1857–1936), a Yugoslavian seismologist, analyzed the seismograms of a Balkan earthquake in 1909. Read about this scientist, and think about these questions:
- What did Mohorovicic discover from the seismograms about the speed of seismic waves at depths around 25 miles (40 km)?
- What is *Moho* short for?

# Bang!

## PROBLEM

*How is the energy of seismic P-waves transmitted through the earth?*

## Materials

scissors
ruler
string
masking tape
5 marbles

## Procedure

1. Cut 5 pieces of string, each 12 inches (30 cm) long.

2. Tape one piece of string to each of the marbles.

3. Tape the free end of each string to the edge of a table. Adjust the position and length of the strings so that the marbles are the same height and touching each other.

4. Pull one of the end marbles to the side, and then release it.

5. Observe any movement of the marbles.

## Results

The marble swings down, striking the closest marble in its path, and stops moving. The marble on the opposite end swings outward, and strikes its closest neighboring marble when it swings back into its original position. The cycle of the end marbles swinging back and forth continues for a few seconds.

## Why?

Raising the end marble gives it energy, which is transferred to the marble it strikes. This energy is passed from one marble to the next, as each marble pushes against the next. The end marble is pushed away from the group. The transfer of energy from one marble to the next simulates the transfer of energy between particles of the earth during a **seismic P-wave** (primary pressure wave of an earthquake).

The first sign that an earthquake has occurred is the hammerlike blow felt and heard as a P-wave exits through the earth's surface. Before that, P-waves move through liquids and solids by **compressing** (pressing together) the particles of earth directly in front of them. The compressed

particles quickly spring back to their original position as soon as the energy moves on. The crust of the earth moves upward as it is hit with the energy of the P-wave, and then settles back into place when the energy moves on.

## LET'S EXPLORE

1. Would it affect the transmission of energy if the marbles were not in line? Stick pieces of clay under the strings on the side of the table in order to change the position of the marbles. Be sure that the marbles touch at some point, but that each marble is at a different height.

2. Would changing the distance between particles affect the transfer of energy? Repeat the original experiment, moving the pieces of tape supporting the marbles farther apart so that there is a slight separation between each marble.

## SHOW TIME!

1. Use a Slinky to demonstrate the particle movement of a seismic P-wave as it moves from the **focus** (starting point) of an earthquake to the **epicenter** (the point on the earth's surface directly above the focus). The Slinky can be used as part of a project presentation by slightly stretching it vertically and attaching its top and bottom loops to the display. Compress four to five loops together at one end, then release.

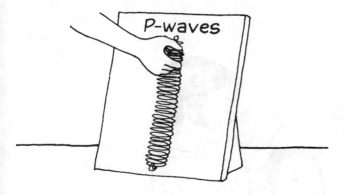

2. Seismic waves move more slowly through sand because the energy of the waves moves forward in different directions as the sand particles move outward in all directions. To demonstrate this, cover the end of a paper towel tube with a paper towel. Secure the paper towel to the tube with a rubber band. Fill the tube with uncooked rice or bird seed. Use your fingers to press down on the rice as you try to push the rice down and out through the paper towel.

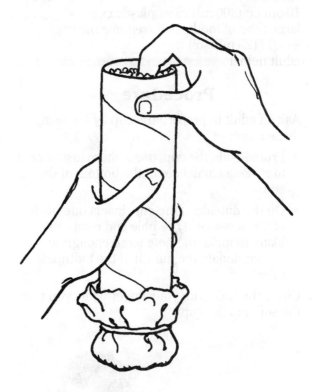

## CHECK IT OUT!

P-waves are the swiftest seismic waves. Find out the speed of P-waves as they travel through the different layers of the earth's interior: crust, mantle, and core. Display a diagram of a cross section of the earth, with speeds of P-waves indicated for each layer.

## PROBLEM

*How does intrusive volcanism (movement beneath the earth's surface) change the shape of the earth's crust?*

## Materials

scissors
10-ounce (300-ml) clear plastic cup
large tube of toothpaste (remove the cap)
½ cup (125 ml) soil
adult helper

## Procedure

1. Ask an adult to prepare the cup by following these steps:

   • From inside the cup, use a sharp instrument to make a small hole in the bottom of the cup.

   • On the outside of the cup, insert one blade of the scissors in the hole and rotate the blade to make the hole large enough to accommodate the mouth of the toothpaste tube.

2. Cover the hole with your finger while you pour the soil into the cup.

3. Insert the mouth of the toothpaste tube into the hole.

4. Ask your helper to hold the cup while you press against the tube to force the toothpaste into the cup.

5. Observe the contents of the cup as the toothpaste enters. Pay special attention to the surface of the soil.

## Results

As the toothpaste rises in the cup, the soil is pushed upward, forming a dome-shaped rise in the soil's surface.

## Why?

Liquid rock beneath the earth's surface is called magma. Pressure on pools of magma deep within the earth forces it toward the surface. Magma that has reached the earth's surface is called **lava**. This movement of magma within the earth is referred to as **intrusive volcanism**. Intrusive volcanism is responsible for different types of **intrusions** (flows of magma that cool and harden before they reach the surface). Intrusions have many shapes because magma hardens in many positions as it cools. Hardened or solidified magma forms **igneous rock**. A dome-shaped intrusion is called a **laccolith**, formed when magma pushes overlying rock upward. The toothpaste simulates the formation of a laccolith. The mushroom-shaped paste pushes the overlying contents of the cup upward, producing a mound on the soil's surface.

## LET'S EXPLORE

What would happen if rock layers restricted the upward movement of the magma? Repeat the experiment, adding rocks to the soil mixture and inserting an empty plastic cup in the cup of soil. Ask your helper to push down on the empty cup to restrict the movement of soil as you force toothpaste into the cup of soil. **Science Fair Hint:** Use the descriptions in Show Time! to identify the type of intrusion formed. Label and display drawings of the models from this and the original experiment.

soil
rocks
toothpaste

## SHOW TIME!

1. Bodies of intrusive igneous rock are classified according to their shape and relationship to surrounding rock. Use the description of each type of rock structure and the diagram to build a clay model showing the rock structures formed by intrusive activities. This model can be used as part of a project display.

   - **Batholiths:** Large intrusions below the earth's surface
   - **Dikes:** Narrow, vertical intrusions that rise and break through horizontal rock layers.
   - **Laccoliths:** Mushroom- or dome-shaped intrusions that push up the overlying rock layers.
   - **Sills:** Thin, horizontal intrusions sandwiched between other rock layers.
   - **Stocks:** Intrusions below the earth's surface that are smaller than batholiths.

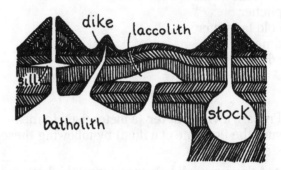

dike    laccolith
sill
batholith    stock

2. Granite is the most common type of intrusive igneous rock. The composition of granite can vary depending on the kinds and proportions of minerals present in the magma that formed it. Purchase different samples of granite at a rock shop, or collect your own samples. Use these as part of a display showing the different shapes of intrusions and their composition.

## CHECK IT OUT!

Domed mountains, such as the Henry Mountains of southern Utah or the Black Hills of South Dakota, are broad, circular mountains formed when layers of rock are lifted. Find out more about the surface landforms created by intrusions. What is the surface like in areas where the different intrusions are exposed when rocks around them are worn away by erosion? Examples of exposed batholiths are the Sierra Nevada mountains of California. Identify other exposed areas created by intrusions.

# 30 Slow Mover

## PROBLEM

*How does the viscosity of lava affect its flow rate?*

## Materials

scissors
empty, clear plastic dishwashing-liquid bottle
   with pull top
ruler
marking pen
modeling clay
jar with a mouth slightly smaller than the base
   of the bottle
pitcher
cold tap water
timer
adult helper

## Procedure

1. Prepare a **viscometer** (a meter used to measure the flow rate of a fluid) by following these steps:

   • Ask your adult helper to cut off the bottom of the bottle.

   • Hold the bottle upside down. The bottom edge of the bottle will now be referred to as the top. Draw two straight, horizontal lines on the bottle: one about 1 inch (2.5 cm) below the open top, and the other 4 inches (10 cm) below the first line.

   • Label the top line Start and the bottom line Stop.

   • Make sure the pull top of the bottle is closed.

   • Place a band of clay around the mouth of the jar.

   • Rest the upside-down bottle on the mouth of the jar. Mold the clay so that the bottle stands upright but is not secured to the clay.

2. Fill the pitcher with cold tap water.

3. Pour the water into the open end of the bottle until the water is about ½ inch (1.25 cm) above the Start line.

4. Lift the bottle and pull the top open.

5. Immediately return the bottle to the mouth of the jar. When the water level reaches the Start line, start the timer.

6. Stop the timer when the water level reaches the Stop line.

7. Record the flow time in seconds.

8. Repeat steps 2 to 7 three times.

clay

START
STOP

VISCOMETER

9. Average the flow time of cold tap water by adding the three flow times together and dividing the sum by 3. The following example shows the author's flow time and the calculated average flow time.

Sum of flow time (seconds)
= 39.2 + 39.4 + 39.3
= 117.9 seconds
Average flow time
= 117.9 seconds ÷ 3
= 39.3 seconds

## Results

The flow time will vary with the shape of the bottle used. The author's average flow time for cold tap water was 39.3 seconds.

## Why?

The amount of time it takes a liquid to flow out of a container depends on its viscosity. The **viscosity** of a liquid is its resistance to flow, or its stickiness. Water has a low viscosity and flows quickly out of the open viscometer.

Different types of lava have different viscosities. Some are so thick and sticky and have such a high viscosity that they creep along, moving only a few yards (m) per day. Others have a low viscosity and flow a few miles (km) per hour.

## LET'S EXPLORE

1. How does the viscosity of other liquids compare to the viscosity of water? Repeat the experiment, using liquids such as oil, dishwashing liquid, honey, and/or syrup. Wash and wipe the viscometer clean with a paper towel after each test, or prepare separate instruments for each liquid tested. Compare the flow times of the liquids.

2. Does the temperature of a liquid affect its viscosity? Repeat the original experiment twice. First, reduce the temperature of the liquids by chilling them in the freezer. Then, heat the liquids by placing a container of each in a bowl of warm tap water. **Science Fair Hint:** Prepare bar graphs to display the results of each liquid tested. Label the results from the original, room-temperature test as the medium temperature.

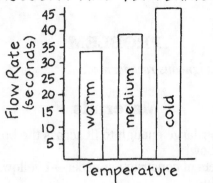

VISCOSITY AND TEMPERATURE

## SHOW TIME!

What happens to the flow rate of lava when it contains particles of a solid? Build two volcanoes out of clay. Make each volcano about 6 inches (15 cm) tall with a small, bowl-shaped indention at the top, and put each in the center of a plate. Pour 1 cup (250 ml) of dishwashing liquid into the indention on the top of one volcano. Observe the flow rate of the liquid as it overflows and runs down the side of the clay mountain. Mix ¾ cup (188 ml) of dishwashing liquid with ¼ cup (63 ml) of sand. Pour this mixture in the top of the second volcano. Again, observe the flow rate of the liquid as it flows down the volcano's sides. Take photographs of the experiments and use them as part of a project display.

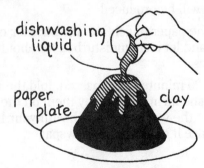

## CHECK IT OUT!

Hot, thin lava flows freely and forms smooth layers when cooled. Cool, thick lava breaks and tumbles forward rather than flows. It produces a rough texture when cooled. Find out more about the movement of lava and its appearance when cooled. Describe *pahoehoe* and *aa*, Hawaiian names for two different types of lava.

# 31 Transformed

## PROBLEM

*How is igneous rock formed?*

## Materials

strainer large enough to fit across the bowl
deep bowl
2 sheets of construction paper—1 yellow,
    1 blue
food blender (to be used only by an adult)
2 cups (500 ml) tap water
1 teaspoon (15 ml) white school glue
timer
10 to 12 sheets of newspaper
adult helper

## Procedure

1. Set the strainer across the mouth of the bowl.

2. Tear each sheet of construction paper into small pieces.

3. Drop the paper pieces into the blender.

4. Add the water and glue to the blender.

5. Ask an adult to turn on the blender and thoroughly mix the paper and water. A thick paper mulch will be produced.

6. Pour the paper mulch into the strainer over the bowl, and let it sit undisturbed for about 20 minutes.

7. When 20 minutes have passed, fold the newspaper sheets in half and lay them on the table. Pick up the wet paper mulch with your hand and place it on top of the newspaper.

8. Allow the paper mulch to dry and solidify. This may take 2 to 3 days.

## Results

The dark greenish gray mulch becomes a lumpy solid.

## Why?

The blending of different-colored paper pieces and water represents the melting of different rocks beneath the surface of the earth due to heat and pressure. This melted rock is called magma. When magma rises to the surface of the earth, it is called lava. Magma and lava cool and solidify to form a type of rock called igneous rock. The drying of the paper mulch represents the cooling of magma or lava to form igneous rock.

## LET'S EXPLORE

1. How is **sedimentary rock** (rock formed by deposits of sediment, or small particles of material deposited by wind, water, or ice) formed from igneous rock? Demonstrate this transformation by repeating the experiment twice, first using yellow and blue paper as in the original experiment, then using white and yellow paper. For ease of handling, work with the paper mulch before it has completely solidified. Break half of the dark mulch into small pieces and press them into a thin layer on top of a stack of newspaper. Make a second layer, using half of the light mulch. Add a third and fourth layer, alternating the dark and light mulches. Allow the model to dry. These two mulches represent two samples of lava. In nature, lava cools and solidifies to form igneous rock. **Weathering** (the breaking down of rock into smaller pieces by natural processes) causes small particles of igneous rock to break off. The particles build up in layers and eventually form sedimentary rock. **Science Fair Hint:** Use the model you made to represent the formation of sedimentary rock.

2. How can **metamorphic rock** (rock formed from other types of rock by pressure and heat) form from sedimentary rock? Demonstrate this transformation by repeating the previous experiment, except that after you've laid the

last layer of mulch, cover it with 2 to 3 sheets of newspaper. In nature, metamorphic rock is formed by pressure applied to rock in solid form. So that you do not have to apply so much pressure, you can work with the layers before they solidify. With a rolling pin, roll back and forth three to four times across the top of the newspaper covering the layers of mulch. Press as hard as you can to try to flatten the layers. Remove the pressed mulch and place it to dry on newspaper. **Science Fair Hint:** Use the model to represent the formation of metamorphic rock.

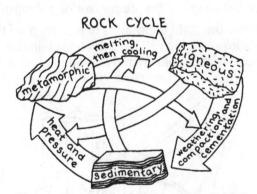

ROCK CYCLE

## SHOW TIME!

1. Rocks come from other rocks. Igneous rock forms when sedimentary or metamorphic rock melts, then cools. Sedimentary rock is made from sediments of metamorphic or igneous rocks. These sediments form as a result of weathering and are deposited in layers. The

layers are compacted and cemented. Metamorphic rock forms when igneous or sedimentary rock is changed by heat and/or pressure. This never-ending process by which rocks change from one type to another is called the **rock cycle**. Draw and display a diagram similar to the one shown to represent the rock cycle.

## CHECK IT OUT!

1. Each rock type can change into either of the other two rock types. Can a rock be changed into a different rock but remain the same type of rock? For example, can granite, an igneous rock, be heated and cooled to form a different kind of igneous rock? Find out and prepare a display showing different possible changes.

2. Heat and pressure can change granite, an igneous rock, into quartzite, a metamorphic rock. Find out more about the rock cycle. Make diagrams like the one shown, showing the names and types of the rocks and how they change.

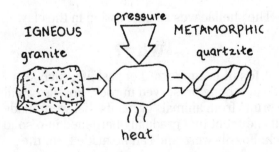

## PROBLEM

*What are fossils?*

## Materials

1-inch (2.5-cm) -thick piece of modeling clay
   with a surface larger than the shell
petroleum jelly
seashell (or small shell-shaped soap)

## Procedure

1. Cover the top surface of the clay with a thin layer of petroleum jelly.
2. Press the outside of the shell firmly into the clay until most of the shell is surrounded by the clay.
3. Gently lift the shell out of the clay.

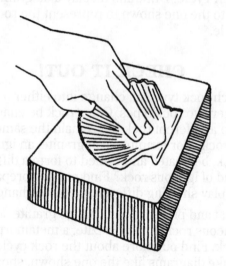

## Results

The shell leaves an impression in the clay.

## Why?

A **fossil** is any record of past life, such as a shell or a bone preserved in rock. Fossils can also be prints from animals or plants that were made in soft sediment that gradually hardened into solid rock. Fossils were and can be made from the remains of an organism buried in sediment. The remains rot away completely as the sediment hardens into rock, leaving in the rock a cavity the size and shape of the organism. This impression of an organism within a rock cavity is called a **fossil mold**.

This experiment represents the formation of a fossil mold. The shell represents the remains of the organism, and the clay represents the soft sediment that will harden into rock. The print left by the shell is a model of a fossil mold.

## LET'S EXPLORE

1. The cavity in which an object can be shaped is called a **mold**. A fossil mold can be used as a mold to create a reproduction of the surface texture of the organism. Repeat the experiment, making another impression of the shell. In a paper cup, mix 2 tablespoons (30 ml) of plaster of paris with 1 tablespoon (15 ml) of tap water, then stir with a craft stick. Fill this mold with the wet plaster. Allow the plaster to dry (about 20 to 30 minutes), then remove the clay. The dried plaster retains the actual surface texture of the original object, the shell. *NOTE: Do not wash the paper cup or the craft stick in the sink, because the plaster can clog the drain.*
2. Under the right conditions in nature, mud that fills fossil molds will harden and retain the shape of the mold. When a mold is filled with a

substance such as mud or plaster that hardens, the result is a solid reproduction of an organism, called a **cast**. Casts have the same outer shape as the organism. Mud casts that change into rock form fossil prints of the organism. Make a mud cast by repeating the previous experiment, but replace the plaster with garden soil. **Science Fair Hint:** Use the mold and cast of the shell as part of a science fair display.

## SHOW TIME!

1. Another way to show how fossil molds form in sedimentary rock is described in Experiment 26, "Imprints." Follow the steps described in the procedure to make an imprint of your hand. Display photographs of the procedure and the results to represent the formation of a mold.

2. How does **metamorphism** (the process by which rock changes from one type to another due to pressure and heat) affect fossils? Use the fossil mold model made in the previous experiment to represent how pressure

changes sedimentary rock into metamorphic rock. Roll a rolling pin back and forth across the hardened mold. Take photographs of the mold before and after applying pressure, and use them to prepare a poster representing the effects of metamorphism. The title of the poster might be "Fossils versus Metamorphism."

## CHECK IT OUT!

1. Fossils are more commonly found in limestone and shale than in sandstone. Find out more about fossils and the rocks in which they are found. Why are fossils found in sedimentary rock but not in igneous or metamorphic rock? What is fossiliferous limestone?

2. Petrified wood forms when silica minerals in groundwater replace wood fibers and/or fill pores in buried wood. Find out more about this process. How long does it take for complete petrification? Where is petrified wood of gem quality found?

# Patterns

## PROBLEM

*How do atoms and molecules arrange themselves in minerals?*

## Materials

large, shallow baking pan
tap water
1 teaspoon (5 ml) dishwashing liquid
spoon
drinking straw

## Procedure

1. Fill the pan half full with water, then add the dishwashing liquid.

2. Gently stir with the spoon to thoroughly mix the liquids without producing any bubbles.

3. Place one end of the straw beneath the surface of the water.

4. Slowly and gently blow through the straw to make a cluster of 5 to 15 bubbles. *CAUTION: Only exhale through the straw. Do not inhale.*

5. Move the straw to a different location and blow a single bubble.

6. With the straw, move the bubble so that it touches the bubble cluster.

7. Move the straw to a different location and blow through the straw as before to make a cluster of 5 to 15 bubbles.

8. With the straw, move one bubble cluster so that it touches the other bubble cluster.

## Results

The single bubble attaches to the bubble cluster. The two clusters of bubbles join, making one cluster.

## Why?

The bubbles represent the chemical particles of a mineral. **Chemical particles** are the **atoms** (the building units of matter) or molecules that make up minerals and all matter. A **mineral** is a solid formed in the earth by nature from sub-

stances that were never a plant or animal. Such substances are said to be **inorganic.** The addition of each bubble to the bubble cluster and the joining of the clusters represent the growth of a mineral **crystal** (a solid made up of atoms arranged in an orderly, regular pattern). Chemical particles, like the bubbles, can move around in a liquid. Just as a single bubble or bubble cluster moves to a place where it fits in the bubble cluster, chemical particles dissolved in a liquid move to just the right spot in order to fit with other particles.

One of the four basic characteristics of minerals is their definite chemical composition with atoms arranged in an orderly, regular pattern. Once a chemical particle, like the bubble, moves into the right place, it is held there by the attraction it has to the other chemical particles. This attraction between like chemical particles is called **cohesion.** The shape and size of the chemical particles determine how they arrange themselves and the pattern they form.

## LET'S EXPLORE

Show how the size of the bubbles affects the results. Repeat the experiment twice, first using a narrower straw, then replacing the straw with a cardboard tube from a paper towel roll. **Science Fair Hint:** As part of a project display, use photographs to represent the arrangement and patterns formed by the different bubble sizes.

## SHOW TIME!

**1a.** Sugar crystals are **organic** (formed from living matter). They are not minerals, but they can be used to represent the ways that crystals in minerals form. Ask an adult to prepare a sugar-gelatin solution by using the following steps:

- Pour ½ cup (125 ml) of distilled water into a small saucepan.

- Sprinkle ¼ ounce (7 g) of unflavored gelatin on the surface of the water and let it stand undisturbed for 2 minutes.

- Stir the liquid continuously over medium heat until the gelatin is completely dissolved.

- Slowly add 1¼ cups (313 ml) of table sugar while stirring.

- Continue to stir until all the sugar is dissolved.

- When the liquid starts to boil, remove the saucepan from the heat.

- Allow the solution to cool for 15 minutes.

- Pour the cooled solution into a 1-pint (500-ml) glass jar.

Place the jar where it can remain undisturbed for at least 2 weeks. Make daily observations and draw diagrams of the jar's contents. Display the diagrams.

**b.** The gelatin provided a surface for the sugar molecules to cling to. Would the molecules cling to other surfaces? Have an adult repeat the previous procedure, omitting the unflavored gelatin. Cut a piece of cotton string slightly longer than the height of the jar. Tie a paper clip to one end of the cotton string. Lower the paper clip into the jar of solution so that the paper clip rests on the bottom of the jar. Tie the free end of the string to the middle of a pencil laid across the opening of the jar. Make daily observations and diagrams of the jar's contents for at least 2 weeks.

## CHECK IT OUT!

Find out more about the formation of minerals. What is a geode? How are geodes formed? What mineral is most often found in geodes?

# Collection

## PROBLEM

*How do you label a mineral collection?*

### Materials

mineral samples (found in your area or purchased from local rock and mineral shops or teaching supply stores. See Appendix C for other sources.)
white typewriter correction fluid with brush
timer
black fine-point permanent marking pen
2 index cards for each mineral sample
2 card file boxes

### Procedure

1. Label each mineral sample by using the following steps:

   - With the brush, paint a small spot of correction fluid on each mineral sample. Place the spot in an unimportant area of the mineral.
   - Wait 2 to 3 minutes to allow the spot to dry.
   - With the marking pen, write a reference number on each spot.

2. Prepare a card file by using the following steps:

   - Write the reference number of each mineral sample on a file card.
   - Write the details of each sample, including the following:
     a. specimen's name
     b. where it was obtained (If found in nature, include information about other minerals or rocks at the location.)
     c. identifying features, such as color, **luster** (shininess), hardness, **cleavage** (the tendency of a mineral to break along a smooth surface), and **streak** (the color of the powder left when a mineral is rubbed against a rough surface that is harder than the mineral). These identifying features can be found in a rock and mineral field guide, such as *The Audubon Society Field Guide to North American Rocks and Minerals* by Charles W. Chesterman (New York: Knopf, 1993) or *Rocks and Minerals* by Chris Pellant (New York: Dorling Kindersley, 1992).
   - Place the cards in one of the card file boxes in numerical order.
   - Prepare a second set of cards with identical information, but place the cards in the other card file box in alphabetical order.

## Results

You've created an index card catalog for a mineral collection.

## Why?

The numbered minerals and the set of numerically ordered index cards make it easy for you to quickly identify each sample in your mineral collection. The second set of cards in alphabetical order allows you to search by name for a specific mineral in your collection and its corresponding reference number.

## LET'S EXPLORE

**1a.** How do you label a rock collection? Repeat the procedure for labeling minerals, but use rock samples and a different color of correction fluid.

**b.** Along with the reference number, place a letter on each rock to identify its class. Use the following letter identification system or design your own: S—sedimentary, M—metamorphic, I—igneous.

**2.** If some of your rocks contain fossils and you wish to keep your fossil collection separate from the rest of your rock collection, repeat the original procedure for labeling minerals, but use fossil samples and a third color of correction fluid.

## SHOW TIME!

**1.** Store your rock and mineral collections in a way that keeps the samples separate from one another. Place the samples in egg cartons or in small boxes arranged on a tray, shallow box, or baking pan. Put cotton beneath each specimen as padding. Place all your rock samples in one carton or on one tray, all your mineral samples in another carton or tray, and use a third carton or tray if you prefer to keep fossil samples separate. Identify your collections with stand-up signs made from index cards folded in half lengthwise and labeled "Rocks," "Minerals," and "Fossils" if included.

**2.** Use a wooden backboard with shelves on each panel as a project display. Display individual

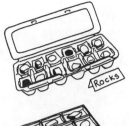

samples with an information card stating important and/or interesting facts about the sample, such as its name, where you found it, and its use. Mention identifying tests, such as hardness and streak tests, on the card. List each mineral's cleavage tendencies. Make some samples of rocks and minerals available so that observers can touch and feel them. Be prepared to answer observers' questions about any and all samples displayed.

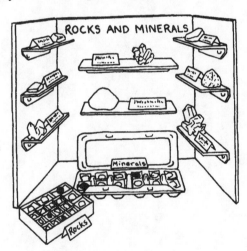

## CHECK IT OUT!

**1.** Identifying tests, such as hardness, streak, and specific gravity, can be determined experimentally. For information about these tests, see pages 20–27 in *Janice VanCleave's Rocks and Minerals* (New York: Wiley, 1996). See Appendix C for sources of rock and mineral samples.

**2.** Use the library to find available rock and mineral books, magazines, and articles. *Rocks & Minerals* magazine is a wonderful resource.

# Engineering

Rounded Domes
Supported ___ lbs. (___ kg)

Pointed Domes
Supported ___ lbs. (___ kg)

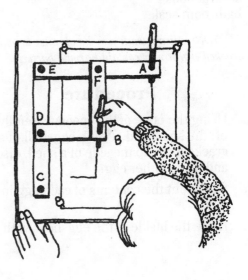

E   A
F
D
B
C

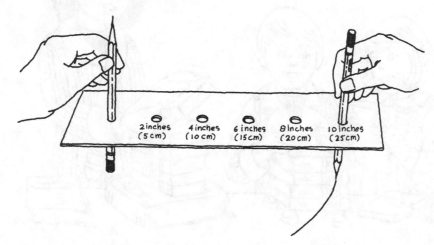

2 inches (5 cm)   4 inches (10 cm)   6 inches (15 cm)   8 inches (20 cm)   10 inches (25 cm)

## PROBLEM

*How does the molecular structure of an eggshell affect its strength?*

### Materials

metal spoon
4 raw eggs in their shells
bowl
tap water
paper towel
masking tape
nail scissors
several books
bathroom scale

*CAUTION: Always wash your hands after touching an uncooked egg. It may contain harmful bacteria.*

### Procedure

1. Using the edge of the spoon, carefully break off the small end of each eggshell. If any cracks form up the side of a shell, discard it and use another egg.

2. Shake out the contents of each egg into the bowl.

3. Rinse the inside of the eggshells with water.

4. Carefully dry the outside of the shells with the paper towel.

5. Wrap a piece of tape around the center of each shell as shown, positioning the tape the same on each shell.

6. Use the nail scissors to cut away the broken ends around the bottom of the tape on each shell.

7. Place the shells, open end down, in a rectangular array on a table.

8. Place one book on top of the shells, and position the shells so that one is under each corner of the book.

9. Carefully add the other books, one at a time, to the book on top of the eggshells, waiting 30 seconds before adding each book. Keep adding books until a cracking sound is heard. Record the number of books required to cause the first crack.

10. Continue to carefully stack the books until one or more of the shells collapse. Record the number of books required to cause the crush.

11. Use the bathroom scale to weigh first the books required to crack a shell and then all of the books required to collapse one or more of the shells.

## Results

The number of books the eggs will hold depends on the weight of each book and the shape of the eggs used. [The author's result was that 5 books weighing 15 pounds (6.8 kg) produced the first crack, and 2 additional, smaller books, bringing the total weight to 19 pounds (8.6 kg), collapsed the eggs.]

## Why?

Eggshells consist largely of the mineral calcium carbonate. The molecules of calcium carbonate are arranged in a dome-shaped structure around the contents of the egg. The weight placed on top of each egg is spread down along the curved sides to the base. No single point on the dome supports the whole weight, so together they can support quite a heavy weight. The dome shape provides a structure imitated by architects because of its strength and ability to span a large area.

## LET'S EXPLORE

Would the eggshells support more or less weight if the small end of the shell was used? Repeat the experiment, but break off the large end of the shell. Record the number and weight of books that caused the first crack and then the number and weight needed to crush the shells. **Science Fair Hint:** As part of a project display, prepare new shells from the large (rounded) and small (pointed) ends of the eggs. Exhibit the shells supporting lightweight books. Label the display with the total amount of weight that each set of eggs can support.

## SHOW TIME!

1. How are molecules arranged in solids? Molecules in solids are not packed tightly together; much space exists in a solid. Explain and diagram how the "holding forces" among the molecules in a solid give it a definite shape and a definite volume and affect its strength.

2. Observe and collect samples of different types of solids. Make comparisons and draw conclusions about the strength of each type of material. Make a list of questions such as these about the samples collected and discover the answers: Are all wooden pieces hard? Can all samples of cloth be easily torn, and does the cloth tear with the same ease in all directions? Do all paper samples have the same strength? Display the samples, a list of your questions, and the answers to each question.

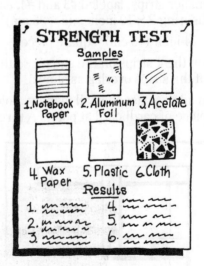

## CHECK IT OUT!

Weight can be successfully hung from some solids but not from others. This is due to the tensile strength of the material. What is tensile strength? Which solids have great tensile strength?

# Enlarger

## PROBLEM

*How does a pantograph work?*

## Materials

scissors
ruler
cardboard box at least 24 inches (60 cm) wide
    and 24 inches (60 cm) high
10d nail
4 paper brads
2 marking pens
4 thumbtacks
large sheet of plain white paper (such as
    butcher paper)
adult helper

## Procedure

1. Ask an adult to cut the following pieces from the cardboard box:

    - 2 strips, labeled #1 and #2, each measuring 2 × 18 inches (5 × 45 cm).

    - 2 smaller strips, labeled #3 and #4, each measuring 2 × 10 inches (5 × 25 cm)

    - one 24-inch (60-cm) -square piece

2. Position the 4 strips on the square so that the ends of the strips overlap as shown.

3. Ask an adult to use the nail to make holes in each piece of cardboard at points A through F,

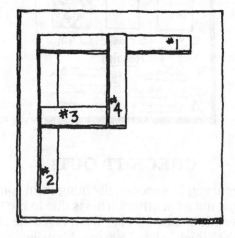

as shown in the diagram. *NOTE: C is the only hole made through the square.*

4. Use paper brads to secure the strips together at points D, E, and F.

5. Use a paper brad to secure strip 2 to the square at point C.

6. Insert the marking pens through holes A and B.

7. Use the thumbtacks to secure a piece of paper to the square under the pens.

8. Holding pen B, draw a square.

9. Compare the sizes of the squares drawn by both pens.

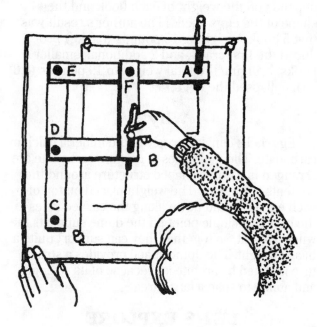

## Results

The square drawn by pen A is larger than that drawn by pen B.

## Why?

A **pantograph**, which is used to change the size of a drawing, is a **compound machine** (a machine made of two or more simple machines) consisting of levers. (Levers are described in Project Idea 4, "Human Machine.") The length of a lever and the position of its fulcrum change the distance that the end of the lever moves; the end farther from the fulcrum moves a greater distance. Strips 1 and 3 are levers with the fulcrum at points E and D. Pen A is farther from its fulcrum than is pen B; thus, pen A is moved a greater distance.

## LET'S EXPLORE

1. Can a reduced-scale drawing be made? Repeat the experiment twice, first using pen A to make the original drawing, then placing pen A in a hole made between points E and F. **Science Fair Hint:** As part of a display, show photographs of the pantograph used in each experiment and display the photos with the drawings.

2. Would connecting the levers at different points affect the results? Repeat the original experiment twice, connecting strip 4 first to the hole made between points E and F in the previous experiment, then to a new hole made between points F and A.

## SHOW TIME!

1. Design your own pantograph, or construct the one shown in the diagram. Place pens at different positions.

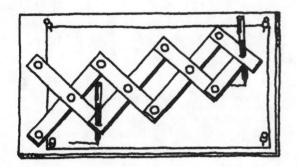

2. A machine that makes circles can further demonstrate that the end of the lever farther from the fulcrum moves a greater distance. Construct a drawing tool by cutting a 2-by-12-inch (5-by-30-cm) strip of cardboard. Use a marking pen to make a dot near one end of the strip. This will be the starting point. With a ruler and a marking pen, mark and label dots every 2 inches (5 cm) from the starting point (see diagram). Ask an adult to use a nail to make a hole through each dot. Place the strip in the center of a sheet of paper. Stand a pencil in the hole at the starting point, with the eraser touching the paper, and hold this pencil steady. To make a circle with a 10-inch (25-cm) diameter, place a second pencil in the hole labeled 10 inches (25 cm) so that its point is pressed against the paper. Move this pencil around until a complete circle is drawn. Repeat, placing the pencil in different holes to change the size of the circle.

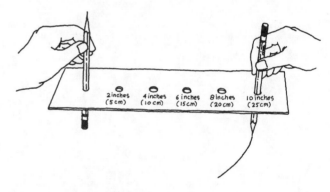

## CHECK IT OUT!

Christopher Scholes (1819–1890) invented the first practical typewriter in 1867. This machine has a series of levers that change a small movement (a fingertip is pressed on a key at one end of the lever) into a larger movement (the other end of the lever goes up and strikes the image of a raised letter onto a piece of paper). Find out more about the connection of the levers in this machine, and display simple diagrams of the connecting levers.

# Physical Science

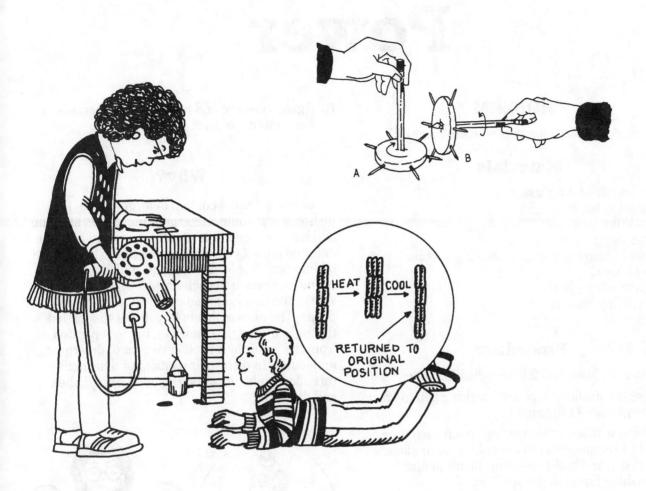

SOLUTIONS

WATER (SOLVENT)

SUGAR (SOLUTE)

WATER + SUGAR (SOLUTION)

DILUTE        CONCENTRATED

# 37

# Cleansing Power

## PROBLEM

*How does dishwashing liquid clean away oil?*

## Materials

4 clear drinking glasses
distilled water
masking tape
marking pen
two 1-teaspoon (5-ml) measuring spoons
cooking oil
dishwashing liquid
4 stirring spoons
timer

## Procedure

1. Fill each glass half full with distilled water.

2. Use the masking tape and marking pen to label the glasses #1 through #4.

3. Using a different measuring spoon each time, add 1 teaspoon (5 ml) of cooking oil to glasses 2 and 4, and add 1 teaspoon (5 ml) of dishwashing liquid to glasses 3 and 4.

4. Place spoons in the glasses.

5. Stir the contents of each glass 25 turns.

6. Observe and record the appearance of the contents of each glass immediately after stirring.

7. Allow the glasses to stand undisturbed for 5 minutes.

8. Again, observe and record the appearance of the contents of each glass.

## Why?

Glasses 3 and 4 contain detergent from the dishwashing liquid. Detergent molecules are long and have one end that attracts water and another end that attracts oil. Stirring the liquid breaks the oil into tiny droplets. Detergent molecules surround and attach to each droplet of oil. The outside of the detergent molecule attaches to water drops. The oil remains in tiny drops suspended throughout the glass of water, but is separated from the water by a protective coat of detergent molecules. In dishwater containing detergent, this allows oily dirt to be removed from dishes and dissolved.

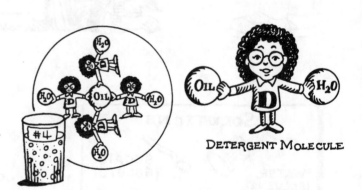

DETERGENT MOLECULE

## Results

| Glass | Contents after Stirring | Contents after Standing 5 Minutes |
| --- | --- | --- |
| #1 | clear | clear |
| #2 | drops of oil swirling throughout the water | circles of oil floating on the water's surface |
| #3 | clear with some foam | clear |
| #4 | cloudy with tiny bubbles floating in water, some foam | cloudy |

## LET'S EXPLORE

Would the amount of dishwashing liquid affect the results? Repeat the experiment, using different amounts of dishwashing liquid.

## SHOW TIME!

1. Is there a difference in the effectiveness of different brands of dishwashing liquids? Repeat the original experiment, using different brands. Take photographs or find advertising pictures of the different products used. Display these pictures with the results chart and the final summary report comparing the effectiveness of the brands.

2. Do shampoos contain detergent? Repeat the previous experiment, replacing the dishwashing liquid with a liquid shampoo. Since the ingredients of shampoos are often kept secret from competitors and consumers, you can only conclude that the cleanser contains a chemical that behaves like a detergent in its ability to break up oils and grease. Make a comparison of the effectiveness of shampoos, and display the results along with a conclusion about the best shampoo as indicated by your testings.

## CHECK IT OUT!

1. Detergent molecules are said to have a split personality because of the different behaviors of each end of the molecule. Find out why one end of the molecule is called hydrophilic and the rest of the molecule is hydrophobic.

2. What are enzymes, and how do enzymatic cleansers cut to pieces protein stains wrapped around the tiny fibers in cloth? What is the source of these stain-snipping enzymes?

# Mixers

## PROBLEM

*Can the addition of sugar to water form a homogeneous mixture?*

## Materials

spoon
drinking glass
dishwashing liquid
tap water
paper towel
distilled water
1 teaspoon (5 ml) sugar
clean drinking straw

## Procedure

*CAUTION: Never taste anything in a laboratory setting unless you are sure that there are no harmful chemicals or materials and that all containers are properly cleaned. This experiment is safe, since only sugar and water are present.*

1. Prepare the materials by washing the spoon and glass in soapy water.

2. Rinse the spoon and glass in clear water, and dry them with the paper towel.

3. Fill the cleaned glass half full with distilled water.

4. Add the sugar to the distilled water.

5. Stir until no sugar particles can be seen.

6. Stand the straw in the glass containing the sugar-water mixture.

7. Collect a sample of the sugar-water mixture by keeping your finger over the top of the straw as you draw the straw out of the glass.

8. Taste the sample and make a mental note of its sweetness.

9. Use the straw to taste samples from the bottom, middle, and top of the sugar-water mixture.

10. Compare the taste of the three samples.

## Results

All three samples have the same sweet taste.

## Why?

In this experiment, sugar is a **solute**, a substance that breaks into smaller parts when dissolved in another substance called a **solvent**—in this case, water. The dissolved particles of a solute move freely throughout the solvent. The combination of a solute with a solvent is called a **solution**. The molecules in the crystals of sugar separate and move between the molecules of water. The sugar-water solution is **homogeneous**, meaning the ratio of sugar molecules to water molecules in the solution is the same throughout. Samples of equal volume taken from the solution contain the same ratio of sugar molecules to water molecules regardless of where the samples were taken.

## LET'S EXPLORE

1. How much sugar will dissolve in water? Use 1 cup (250 ml) of distilled water. Add 1 teaspoon (5 ml) of sugar at a time, stirring after each addition until all the sugar dissolves. Continue to add and record measured amounts of sugar to the water until the particles stop dissolving no matter how much you stir. A solution that will not dissolve any more solute is said to be a **saturated solution**.

2. Would the amount of sugar needed to make a saturated solution change if the water were not distilled? Repeat the original experiment, using tap water.

3. Does the temperature of the water affect the amount of sugar that will dissolve? Repeat the original experiment three times, using ice water, cold tap water, and warm tap water. Place a thermometer in the water and record the temperature. Remove the thermometer before adding the sugar. **Science Fair Hint:** You can use a data chart like the one shown to record and display the temperature of each liquid and the amount of sugar needed to produce a saturated solution.

## SHOW TIME!

1. Make a diagram such as the one shown to explain the following terms: *solute, solvent, solution, dilute, concentrated, saturated,* and *unsaturated.*

2. Solutions are mixtures in which a substance is dissolved in another substance. The sugar-water solution is an example of a solid dissolved in a liquid. Learn about and display other types of solutions such as:

- a gas dissolved in a liquid (soda)
- a gas dissolved in a gas (air)
- a liquid dissolved in a gas (water in air)

## CHECK IT OUT!

A solid dissolved in a solid is called an *alloy.* When metals are mixed together, their properties change. Brass is an alloy of zinc and copper. It is harder and lasts longer than either zinc or copper alone. Alloys are used instead of pure metal because of their special properties. Find out more about alloys such as brass, bronze, pewter, and alnico. What are their special properties, and how are they used?

## SATURATED SOLUTIONS
### Temperature versus Amount of Solute

| Temperature | | | Amount of Solute (Sugar) | | |
|---|---|---|---|---|---|
| cold | _____ °F | (_____ °C) | _____ tsp | (_____ ml) |
| moderate | _____ °F | (_____ °C) | _____ tsp | (_____ ml) |
| warm | _____ °F | (_____ °C) | _____ tsp | (_____ ml) |

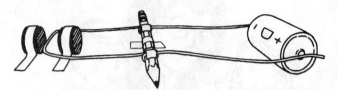

## PROBLEM

*How does a magnet produce movement in a current-carrying wire?*

### Materials

2 small disk magnets
duct tape
18-inch (45-cm) piece of uninsulated 18-gauge wire
pencil
size D battery
adult helper

*CAUTION: When doing the experiments in this project, use ONLY batteries; NEVER use the main electricity supply—it can produce a shock that can kill you. DO NOT hold the wire against the battery terminals longer than 1 second. The wire can get hot and burn your fingers.*

### Procedure

1. Place the magnets on a *wooden* table, leaving a space of about ⅜ inch (1 cm) between them, so that the north pole of one magnet faces the south pole of the other magnet. (The magnets attract each other in this position.)

2. Tape the magnets to the table as shown in the diagram.

3. Wrap the wire around each end of the pencil, leaving about 4 inches (10 cm) of wire free at each end. Secure the wire to the pencil with tape, leaving 2 inches (5 cm) of space between the two wrappings. This makes a loop of wire on one side of the pencil.

4. Lay the pencil on the table so that the free ends of the wire are on one side of the pencil and the loop of wire is between, but not touching, the magnets. Secure the pencil to the table with tape. The loop should be slightly above the table surface.

5. Place the battery between the free ends of the wire and parallel to the pencil.

6. Wrap tape around 1 inch (2.5 cm) of both ends of the wire. Holding the tape, simultaneously touch the bare wire to both battery terminals

(positive and negative), then immediately remove the wire from the battery. Observe any movement in the loop of the wire.

### Results

The loop of wire jerks either up or down, depending on the orientation of the battery terminals.

### Why?

A flow of **electrons** (negatively charged particles of an atom) produces an **electric current**. Electrons move more easily through materials called **electric conductors**, such as copper and other metals. When a **direct current** (a current that flows in one direction) flows through a conductor, such as the copper wire, a magnetic field is produced around the wire. If the current-carrying wire is placed in a magnetic field such as that between the north and south poles of two magnets, the two magnetic fields oppose each other. The result is a force that tends to expel the wire out of the magnetic field between the two magnets. This movement is known as the **motor effect**.

### LET'S EXPLORE

1. Does the direction of the current affect the results? Repeat the experiment, reversing the direction of the battery terminals. **Science Fair Hint:** Electrons flow from the negative

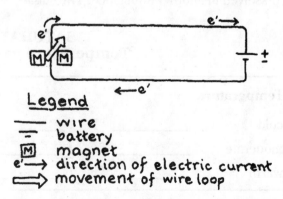

Legend
— wire
— battery
M magnet
e'→ direction of electric current
⇨ movement of wire loop

terminal end of the battery, through the wire, to the positive terminal of the battery. Draw diagrams showing the direction of the current. Use arrows to indicate the movement of the wire. Include a legend for each part of the diagram, as shown.

2. What effect does the strength of the battery have on the results? Repeat the original experiment, using 2 batteries. To connect 2 batteries, hold the positive terminal of one battery against the negative terminal of the other battery and wrap duct tape around the batteries to hold the connection.

3. What effect does the distance between the magnets have on the results? Repeat the original experiment twice, first increasing the distance between the magnets, then decreasing the distance between them.

## SHOW TIME!

In the original experiment, the north pole of one magnet faced the south pole of the other magnet. Construct an instrument that identifies the poles of the magnets by following these steps:
- Cut an L shape from a piece of stiff paper such as poster board. See the diagram for dimensions and labeling.
- Make a hole in the elbow of the instrument with a one-hole paper punch.
- With the back of the instrument facing you, insert the point of the pencil through the hole and away from you. Stand the pencil between the magnets on one of the diagrams on these

pages so that its plus sign (+) points in the same direction as the positive terminal of the battery. Depending on the setup of the battery, either the front or the back of the instrument will be faceup. The arrow by the plus sign on the instrument will point in the direction that the electric current flows, and the arrow by the S on the instrument will point to the south pole of the magnet. The point of the pencil will point in the direction that the wire jerks when the wires touch the battery (up or down). Make a diagram showing how the instrument works.

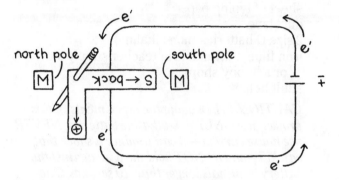

## CHECK IT OUT!

Hans Christian Oersted (1777–1851), a Danish scientist, made a very important discovery while giving a lecture demonstration in 1820. Find out more about Oersted and the experiment that proved that an electric current moving through a wire produces magnetism. You may wish to repeat Oersted's experiment and display diagrams of its results.

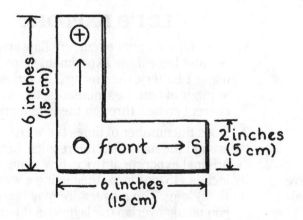

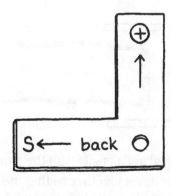

# 40 Attractive

## PROBLEM

*Can electricity produce a magnet?*

## Materials

wire cutters (to be used only by an adult)
ruler
1 yard (1 m) 18-gauge wire
16d steel nail
2 pencils
sheet of typing paper
duct tape
2 size D batteries (non-alkaline)
iron filings (available in teacher supply stores
   or a hobby shop)
adult helper

*CAUTION: When doing the experiments in this project, use ONLY non-alkaline batteries; NEVER use house current—it can produce a shock that can kill you. DO NOT hold the wire against the battery terminals longer than 10 seconds. The wire can get hot and burn your fingers.*

## Procedure

1. Ask an adult to use the wire cutters to strip 2 inches (5 cm) of insulation from both ends of the wire.

2. Wrap the insulated part of the wire tightly around the nail, leaving about 6 inches (15 cm) of wire free on each end.

3. Lay the wrapped nail on a *wooden* table and lay the pencils perpendicular to the nail, one at each end.

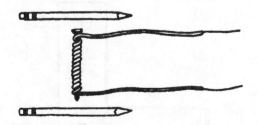

4. Cover the nail and pencils with the paper.

5. Tape the batteries together so that the positive terminal of one touches the negative terminal of the other.

6. Touching the insulated part of the wire, hold the bare ends to the ends of the connected batteries.

7. While the wires are touching the battery terminals, ask your helper to sprinkle iron filings on the paper above the nail and tap the paper gently. Observe the pattern formed.

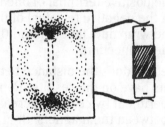

## Results

The iron filings form a pattern of lines around the nail.

## Why?

All wires that carry a direct current are surrounded by a steady magnetic field. When an electric current flows through a coil of wire, the whole coil acts like a magnet. This type of magnet is called an **electromagnet**. Winding the wire into a coil increases the strength of the magnetic field around the electromagnet. The iron nail becomes magnetized by the magnetic field around the wire, adding to the strength of the electromagnet. The iron filings are attracted by the electromagnet, and they line up in the direction of its magnetic field, forming a pattern. (See Experiment 20, "Mapping," for another experiment with magnetic fields.)

## LET'S EXPLORE

1. Would the amount of current flow affect the results? Repeat the experiment twice, first using 1 battery, then using 3 batteries. As the number of batteries increases, the amount of current passed through the wire increases.

2. Does the number of times the wire is wrapped around the nail affect the results? Repeat the original experiment twice, first using a wire 18 inches (45 cm) long, then using a wire 6 feet (2 m) long. The longer wire may require that you neatly overlap the layers on the nail. Be

sure to wrap all the wire in the same direction. **Science Fair Hint:** Make a print of the iron filings pattern by spraying a fine mist of white vinegar over the iron filings on the paper. Leave the paper undisturbed for several hours to allow the iron to rust. Turn the paper over and brush the rusty filings into the trash. The rusty marks leave a pattern of the magnetic field on the paper, which can be displayed as part of your project.

3. Does the size of the core that the wire is wrapped around affect the results? Repeat the original experiment twice, first using a slender nail, then using a thick nail.

upward and cling to the nail tip. Determine the number of BBs that can be lifted from different heights.

b. Compare the strengths of different electromagnets. Repeat the previous experiment twice, first using a wire ½ yard (0.5 m) long, then using a wire 2 yards (2 m) long. As in the previous experiment, neatly overlap the excess wire and wrap it all in the same direction. Use a data chart similar to the one shown to record the wire length, the number of times the wire is wrapped around the nail, the distance from the nail tip to the BBs, and the number of BBs picked up.

## SHOW TIME!

1a. How strong is an electromagnet? Build the original electromagnet, using 1 battery. With clay, stand a ruler next to a saucer of BBs. Touch the bare wires to the battery ends and cover each end with 4 layers of duct tape. Press against the tape to hold the wires securely in place. Slowly lower the nail until BBs move

## CHECK IT OUT!

A coil of wire in a spiral form through which electricity flows is called a *solenoid*. Direct current, or DC, flowing through a solenoid produces an electromagnet. Find out more about electromagnets. Would an electromagnet be produced if alternating current, or AC, flowed through a solenoid? What are some of the uses of electromagnets?

| ELECTROMAGNET STRENGTH | | | |
|---|---|---|---|
| **Wire Length** | **Number of Times Wire Is Wrapped** | **Distance from BBs** | **Number of BBs Picked Up** |
| ½ yard (0.5 m) | | | |
| 1 yard (1 m) | | | |
| 2 yards (2 m) | | | |

# Stretchy

## PROBLEM

*How does heat affect the movement of molecules in a rubber band?*

## Materials

pencil
5-ounce (150-ml) paper cup
scissors
ruler
string
rubber band about 3 inches (7.5 cm) long
salt
masking tape
blow-dryer (to be used only by an adult)
adult helper

## Procedure

1. Use the pencil to punch two opposite holes under the rim of the paper cup.

2. Cut an 8-inch (20-cm) piece of string.

3. Tie the ends of the string through each hole in the cup to form a handle.

4. Cut the rubber band to make a 6–inch (15-cm) strip.

5. Tie one end of the rubber band to the handle of the cup.

6. Cut an 18-inch (45-cm) piece of string, and attach it to the free end of the rubber band.

7. Fill the cup about half full with salt.

8. Set the cup on the floor under the edge of a table.

9. Holding the free end of the string on the edge of the table, slowly pull the string toward the center of the table. When the cup is just resting on the floor, tape the string to the top of the table.

10. Ask an adult to hold the blow-dryer, set to high heat, about 2 inches (5 cm) from the rubber band and move it up and down the band.

11. Observe the position of the cup as the rubber band is heated for about 10 seconds.

12. Remove the heat, and observe the cup for about 20 seconds.

## Results

The cup rises slightly off the floor when the rubber band is heated and returns to its original position as the rubber cools.

## Why?

Heating the rubber band causes the rubber molecules to vibrate. The moving molecules

STRING

RUBBER BAND

STRING

separate slightly and slip past each other, causing the band to thicken and become shorter.

## LET'S EXPLORE

1. Does the size of the rubber band change the movement of the cup? Repeat the experiment, using bands of various thicknesses. Place a yardstick (meterstick) beside the hanging cup to measure any difference in the movement of the cup. **Science Fair Hint:** Make diagrams to show the results and display them with the rubber bands.

2. Does the weight of the cup affect the movement of the heated rubber band? Repeat the original experiment, using measured amounts of salt in the cup. Record the amounts of salt and the distances the cup moved when the rubber band was heated.

## SHOW TIME!

Do all solid materials **contract** (draw together) when heated? Replace the rubber band with a 22-gauge metal wire of comparable length. (Ask an adult to remove any insulation from the wire.) Try using other solid materials. The results from this experiment will indicate that the contraction of the rubber band when heated is contrary to the reaction of most heated materials. Heating generally causes molecules to spread apart, and thus the object expands. Include this information in your report, and use photographs of each of the experiments as part of the project display.

## CHECK IT OUT!

1. Why are bridges, roads, and sidewalks made in sections separated by cracks?
2. Why does heating the metal lid on a jar with warm water make the lid easier to remove?

# Spool Racer

## PROBLEM

*How can a rubber band transform energy?*

### Materials

rubber band (slightly longer than the thread
    spool)
empty thread spool
2 round toothpicks
masking tape
¼-inch (0.63-cm) flat metal washer

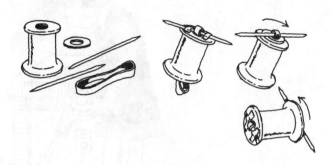

### Procedure

1. Insert the rubber band through the hole in the spool.

2. Put one toothpick through the loop of rubber band at one end of the spool.

3. Center the toothpick in the loop and secure it to the spool with tape on both sides of the rubber band. Do not tape over the rubber band. Break both ends of the toothpick so that they do not extend past the edge of the spool.

4. At the other end of the spool, thread the rubber band through the hole in the washer.

5. Put the second toothpick through the loop in the rubber band. Do not attach this toothpick to the spool.

6. Hold the spool securely with one hand, and with the index finger of your other hand, turn the unattached toothpick around and around in a clockwise direction to wind the rubber band tightly.

7. Place the spool on a flat, smooth surface, such as the floor, and let go.

8. Observe the movement of the spool, rubber band, and toothpicks.

### Results

As the rubber band unwinds, the toothpick taped to the spool turns, turning the spool. The unattached toothpick next to the washer does not turn and is dragged across the surface as the turning spool moves forward.

### Why?

Energy is the capacity to do **work** (the results of a force moving an object). Energy never disappears; it is simply **transformed** (changed from one form to another). **Mechanical energy** is the energy of moving objects. There are two basic forms of mechanical energy: **kinetic energy** (energy of motion), and **potential energy** (stored energy). The rubber band had no energy before it was twisted. It took energy stored in the muscles of your body to wind the rubber band. As long as you held the toothpick, preventing the rubber band from turning, the energy was stored (potential). Releasing the toothpick allowed the rubber band to unwind; thus, the stored energy in the twisted rubber band was transformed into kinetic energy. Machines like the spool (a wheel) do not have energy and can only perform work (move from one place to another) if supplied with energy.

### LET'S EXPLORE

1. Does the number of turns of the rubber band affect the results? Repeat the experiment exactly as before, counting the number of turns made on the rubber band. Then repeat the experiment two more times, first winding the rubber band more turns, then winding it fewer turns.

2. Does the length of the rubber band affect the speed of the moving spool? Repeat the original experiment, using different lengths of rubber bands. Record the rubber band lengths and your results. **Science Fair Hint:** Display the models made with the different lengths of rubber band.

3. Would using sticks smaller or larger than the toothpick change the results? Repeat the original experiment, first using materials of different sizes, such as long and short craft sticks. Then, make the two sticks different lengths.

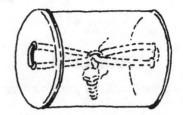

strate the energy produced by an unwinding rubber band. Have an adult construct this can by punching two holes, ½ inch (1.25 cm) apart, in the center of the bottom of a metal can, such as an empty coffee can, and two similar holes in the plastic lid. Thread one rubber band through the holes in the can and a second rubber band through the holes in the lid. Tie the free ends of the rubber bands together with a piece of string, and in the same place tie a heavy bolt. Secure the lid on the can, and roll it forward. The weight of the bolt keeps the rubber bands in place, causing them to wind as the can rolls. As the twisted bands unwind, the can rolls in the opposite direction.

## SHOW TIME!

1. As any rubber band unwinds, its potential energy is changed to mechanical energy. Demonstrate this change by constructing and flying a rubber-band-powered model airplane. Display the model airplane along with photographs taken during a test flight.

2. A can that rolls forward, stops, and mysteriously rolls backward can be used to demon-

## CHECK IT OUT!

Work is accomplished when a force is applied to move an object from one place to another. *Power* is the rate of doing work. *Horsepower* is a unit commonly used to measure power. James Watt (1736–1819), a Scottish engineer and inventor, coined the word *horsepower*. Find out how much power 1 horsepower equals, and why Watt used the term.

# 43 Taller

## PROBLEM

*How does gravity affect a person's height?*

## Materials

scissors
2-liter soda bottle with cap
5 empty plastic thread spools
ruler
string
bowl large enough to hold the soda bottle
tap water
helper
adult helper

## Procedure

1. Have an adult cut the bottom from the bottle.

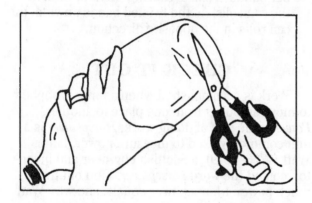

2. Remove any paper covering from the ends of the thread spools.

3. Cut an 18-inch (45-cm) piece of string.

4. Place the string in the bottle so that about 2 inches (5 cm) of string hangs out of the mouth of the bottle.

5. Secure the cap on the bottle, leaving part of the string hanging out.

6. Turn the bottle upside down, then thread the free end of the string through the holes in the spools so that they slide down the string and stand end to end inside the soda bottle.

7. Set the inverted bottle in the bowl.

8. Support the bottle in an upright position with one hand, and hold the string with your other hand so that the spools stand straight.

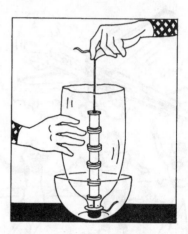

9. Compare the top of the top spool with the top of the bottle. Notice the position of each spool.

10. Ask a helper to fill the plastic bottle with water while you continue to hold the string up.

11. Again, compare the top of the top spool with the top of the bottle. Notice the position of each spool.

## Results

Without the water, the spools stand tightly on top of each other. When the bottle is filled with water, the spools float upward, and there is some separation between spools. The top of the top spool is lower in the empty bottle than it is in the bottle full of water.

## Why?

Without the water, gravity pulls the spools downward, causing them to stand tightly against each other. The water pushes up on the spools. This upward force exerted by a fluid on an object in the fluid is called **buoyancy**, and thus the water simulates a low-gravity environment that reduces the downward pull of gravity. With less downward pull, the spools are allowed to move around more freely. They do not move away from each other because of the connecting string.

The human backbone resembles the stack of spools in that the separate disks that make up the backbone are free to move apart, as are the spools. Like the spools, the backbone has a cord, called the **spinal cord**, that runs through the center of the disks. Gravity pulls the disks down against each other. In space, the discs separate, and the backbone gets longer because gravity is not pulling it down. Astronauts in space are taller than they are on earth.

## LET'S EXPLORE

What would happen if the spools were connected? Cut a strip of cloth about 2 inches (5 cm) wide and 1 inch (2.5 cm) longer than the height of the stacked spools. Attach the ends of the cloth to the top and bottom spools with duct tape. Repeat the experiment. The cloth strip represents **ligaments** (tough bands of tissue connecting the ends of bones) that limit the separation of the disks in the backbone. **Science Fair Hint:** Display the spools with the attached cloth strip along with diagrams and a printed copy of the results.

## SHOW TIME!

1. How does gravity affect pulse rate? One way to simulate an increase in gravity is to add weight to the body. Compare the difference in your pulse rate before and after a 2-minute walk. Carry a heavy backpack and repeat the experiment. Which walk caused a greater increase in pulse rate? Ask volunteers to repeat the experiment, and keep records of their pulse rates before and after each walk. This information can be graphed and used as part of a project display.

2. Does your heart pump as hard as a giraffe's? Make a heart pump as shown in the diagram. Connect straws with duct tape to equal the measurement from the top of your head to the position in which your heart lies in your chest. Squeeze the pump with your hands until the liquid in the bottle rises out of the top straw. Make another pump, building a 6-foot (2-m) straw to represent a blood vessel leading from a giraffe's heart to its head, and squeeze the bottle as before. Compare the amount of effort needed to pump the liquid up both straw "blood vessels." Take photographs to use along with the actual pumps and straw "vessels" as part of a project display. Prepare a written summary of the results.

## CHECK IT OUT!

Astronauts discovered that a "weightless" environment caused many changes in their bodies. Some of the changes took days, and others were apparent within minutes. Find out why the following changes occurred when there was a reduced pull of gravity on the astronauts' bodies:

- Bones lost calcium
- Kidneys worked harder
- There was excess fluid in the face and chest.
- Muscles shrank.
- Heart shrank.

For information, read the article titled "Hang Time for Humans" in *Super Science* magazine, February 1990, Blue Edition, Scholastic Inc.

# Blowing Bubbles

## PROBLEM

*How does gravity affect the shape of soap bubbles?*

## Materials

¼ cup (63 ml) dishwashing liquid
small bowl
¼ cup (63 ml) tap water
spoon
1 teaspoon (5 ml) sugar
large empty thread spool

## Procedure

*NOTE: This is an outdoor experiment.*

1. Pour the dishwashing liquid into the bowl.
2. Add the water to the bowl.
3. Stir the sugar into the soapy mixture to give strength to the bubbles.
4. Dip one end of the thread spool into the mixture.
5. Place your mouth against the dry end of the spool, and gently blow through the hole.

6. Blow a large bubble, and then place your finger over the hole you blew through to prevent the air from leaking out of the soap bubble.
7. Study the bubble's shape until it breaks.
8. Observe and record any movement on the surface of the bubble.

## Results

A bubble that is slightly pointed on the bottom hangs from the spool. Tiny, threadlike streams of liquid quickly swirl down the sides of the bubble and collect at the bottom, where they form drops and fall.

## Why?

The molecules of dishwashing liquid and water link together to form a thin skin of stretchy liquid around the air blown into it. Gravity pulls the rounded bubble downward, forming a slight point at the bottom. Excess liquid on the edge of the spool is pulled down to the lowest point, collects in drops, and drips from the bottom of the bubble. The molecules that make up the thin film of the bubble are also pulled downward, causing the bubble's skin to become thinner at the top until it finally breaks.

## LET'S EXPLORE

1. Does the size of the bubble affect its shape? Blow a large bubble and leave the hole in the top of the spool open to allow the air to leak out. Observe and record any changes in shape as the bubble decreases in size.

2. *G* is the symbol used to rate the force of gravity. The earth's gravity is used as a standard and given the value of 1 G. Pulling the spool upward quickly increases the G-force on the bubble. Determine the shape of a bubble blown where the G-force is greater than that on the earth by blowing a bubble and observing its shape as you move the spool quickly upward. Repeat the procedure, using different upward speeds. **Science Fair Hint:** Record the results and make drawings of the shapes of the bubbles. Use these as part of a project display.

3. Does the shape of the opening in the spool affect the bubble's shape? Would a square or triangular opening make flat-sided bubbles and thus change the effect that gravity might have on the bubble? Use wire to make openings of different shapes; then use them to blow bubbles.

## SHOW TIME!

1. Take photographs while bubbles are being blown from the different-shaped openings and display them along with the written results of the shape produced.

2. What shape would a soap bubble be in space? In space, the pull of gravity is so weak that scientists call it **microgravity**. Everything in space is virtually weightless. Find out the shape of drops of liquids released in a spacecraft, and make drawings of the shape of bubbles in and out of a strong gravitational field. Use these drawings as part of a project display.

## CHECK IT OUT!

Some objects made on the earth have flaws created by the pull of gravity. How does gravity negatively affect the shaping of things like marbles or ball bearings? Make a survey of materials that are difficult to make perfectly round because of gravity. Would these things be easier to make in a spacecraft?

# 45 Toothy

## PROBLEM

*How do gears affect each other's speed and direction of motion?*

## Materials

modeling clay
12 round toothpicks
2 pencils

## Procedure

1. Slightly flatten 2 walnut-size balls of clay to make 2 wheels.

2. Stick 6 toothpicks into the sides of each clay wheel. Be sure the toothpicks are evenly spaced around the clay pieces.

3. Make gear A by pushing a pencil through the center of one clay wheel. Work the pencil around in the hole so that the clay wheel turns easily around the pencil.

4. Make gear B by inserting the other pencil through the center of the second clay wheel. Squeeze the clay around the pencil so that the clay piece and the pencil turn together.

5. Place gear A on a table so that its clay wheel lies flat. Hold the pencil vertically to keep the gear in place.

6. Place gear B next to gear A so that its toothpicks are between those of gear A and perpendicular to them. Hold the pencil horizontally.

7. Rotate the pencil of gear B by turning it away from you.

8. Observe the direction of movement of gear A.

## Results

As gear B rotates vertically, its toothpicks move away from you. They push against the toothpicks of gear A, causing gear A to rotate horizontally. The toothpicks of gear A move toward you. The direction of movement of gear A is opposite to that of gear B.

## Why?

A **gear** is a wheel with teeth around its outer rim. When the teeth of two gears fit together and one gear turns, it causes the other gear to turn. In this experiment, the toothpicks in the clay wheels act as gear teeth. When the gears are of equal size and have the same number of gear teeth, as in this experiment, they both turn at the same speed, but in different directions.

## LET'S EXPLORE

1. Would the number of toothpicks affect the results? Repeat the experiment twice, first placing 4 toothpicks in each clay wheel, then placing 8 toothpicks in each clay wheel. Make an effort to turn gear B at the same speed for both experiments.

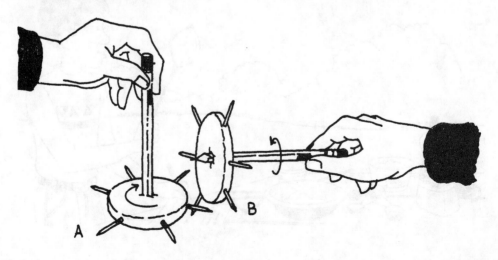

2. Would a different number of gear teeth in each wheel affect the results? Repeat the original experiment, placing 8 toothpicks in the first wheel and 4 toothpicks in the second wheel. In order for the gear teeth to fit together, break the 4 toothpicks used in the second wheel in half, so that the distance between the gears of both wheels is nearly the same. Color one of the toothpicks on each wheel to make it easier to count the turns of each wheel.

## SHOW TIME!

1. Construct a model of gears with different numbers of teeth to demonstrate how gears change the speed of parts being moved. Trace the gear wheels in the diagram on a sheet of paper. Glue the paper to a piece of cardboard, and cut out the gears with scissors. Place the gears on a second piece of cardboard, fitting the gear teeth together. Insert a small nail through the center of each gear, securing the gears to the cardboard so that they turn around easily. Determine the direction that each gear turns and the number of times the small gear turns when the large gear turns once.

2. Use an eggbeater to demonstrate how gears determine the speed and direction of movement. Use a small piece of tape to mark one blade and the wheel so that you can count the turns of the wheels easily.

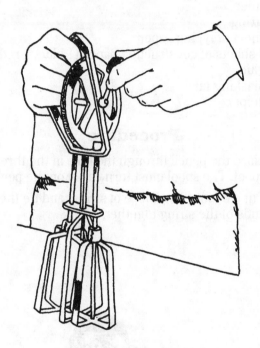

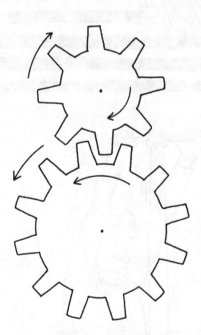

## CHECK IT OUT!

There are four major types of gears: spur gears, rack-and-pinion gears, worm gears, and bevel gears. Find out how each gear type regulates the speed and direction of motion.

# 46 Flag Raiser

## PROBLEM

*How does a fixed pulley make work easier?*

### Materials

pencil (must be small enough to slide through
  the hole in the thread spool)
large, empty thread spool
scissors
ruler
string
sheet of typing paper
2 sheets of construction paper (1 blue, 1 red)
glue
masking tape
helper

### Procedure

1. Place the pencil through the hole in the thread spool. The spool must turn easily on the pencil.

2. Cut a 6-foot (2-m) piece of string, and tie the ends of the string together.

3. Use the following steps and diagram to make a small American flag.

   • Cut the sheet of typing paper in half. Set one of the pieces aside, and cut some stars out of the other piece.

   • Cut a 3-inch (7.5-cm) square from the sheet of blue construction paper. Glue this square in the upper left-hand corner of the white paper, and glue the stars to the blue paper.

   • Cut 6 red strips of paper about ½ inch (1.25 cm) wide, and glue them to the paper, as in the diagram.

4. Tape the star end of the flag to the string.

5. Place the loop of string over the spool so that the flag hangs at the bottom of the loop.

6. Ask a helper to hold the ends of the pencil in both hands at arm's length over his or her head.

7. Pull down on the left side of the loop.

8. Observe the distance the string is pulled down and the distance and direction the flag moves.

## Results

The length of string pulled down over the spool equals the distance the flag moves upward.

## Why?

A **pulley** is a simple machine that consists of a grooved wheel which is turned by a rope or belt. A **fixed pulley** is a pulley that stays in place as it turns. The cord moves over the wheel, and a load is raised as the cord is pulled. The spool is a fixed pulley that allows you to pull down on the string and raise the flag upward. Placing a fixed pulley at the top of a tall flagpole makes the job of raising a flag easier than if you had to carry the flag up the pole. A fixed pulley makes work easier by changing the direction of the effort force (the force applied).

## LET'S EXPLORE

Would the size of the spool affect the results? Repeat the experiment twice, first using a smaller spool, then using a larger spool. If the smaller spool does not easily turn around on the pencil, replace the pencil with a rod of smaller diameter.

## SHOW TIME!

1. Build a movable clothesline using 2 thread spools, 2 large paper clips, and string. You can do this directly on a project backboard. Unbend each paper clip into the shape of a square, then straighten out the shortest side so that the paper clip has three sides at right angles to each other. Slip the spool onto the longest wire of the paper clip, then bend the wire down into the square shape again. Position the spools across from each other on the display and tape the paper clips to the display so that the spools stand upright. Place a loop of string between the spools. Use small clothespins or bobby pins to attach doll clothes to the clothesline. Pull the string to demonstrate the use of the fixed pulleys to move the clothes from one side of the display to the other.

2. A pulley that raises bricks to the top of a building is a fixed pulley. Find out more about fixed pulleys, and display pictures of their uses.

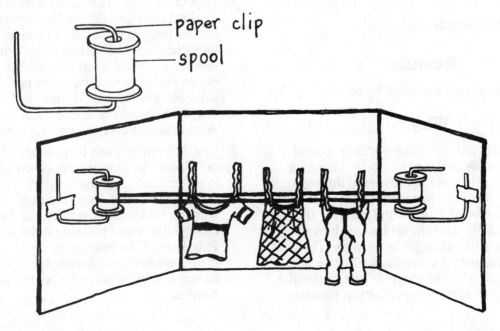

paper clip
spool

# Eraser

## PROBLEM

*How do magnets affect tape recordings?*

### Materials

blank cassette tape
cassette recorder
strong magnet
pencil
helper

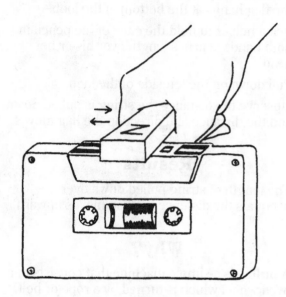

### Procedure

1. Place the cassette tape in the recorder.

2. Record your voice on the cassette tape.

3. Rewind the tape in the recorder and listen to your voice.

4. Remove the cassette from the recorder.

5. Ask your helper to use the pencil to rewind the cassette while you rub the magnet against the tape as it passes the opening in the side of the tape case. Continue until the tape is completely rewound.

6. Place the cassette back in the recorder and replay it.

7. Observe the sounds produced.

### Results

Most or all of your voice will be erased.

### Why?

The cassette tape is a magnetic strip wound around two spools enclosed in a case. Tiny magnetic particles are randomly scattered throughout the tape. The magnetic particles form no particular pattern on a blank tape. Sound entering the microphone of the machine is changed into an electric current that changes in strength. The current moves magnets that are inside the machine, and the movement of the magnets rearranges the magnetic particles on the tape. Certain positions of the magnetic particles produce the sound of your voice. Rubbing the tape with a magnet causes the magnetic material to be pushed and pulled out of place. Rearranging the magnetic particles erases the sound of your voice. Magnetic recording tapes should be kept away from magnets.

### LET'S EXPLORE

1. How close does the magnet have to be in order to affect the tape? Repeat the experiment, placing the magnet at different distances from the tape. **Science Fair Hint:** Demonstrate the erasing of a voice from the cassette tape during an oral presentation of the project. Record someone's voice, play it back, and then use the magnet to erase the sound. Describe what the magnet is doing as you rub it across the tape.

2. Can different sounds be produced by the magnet? Move the magnet around on a blank tape in order to arrange the magnetic particles in different patterns. Experiment to determine whether different movements of the magnet change the sound pattern on the tape. **Science Fair Hint:** Take photographs of each step of the experiment and display them with brief descriptions of what is happening and the results.

## SHOW TIME!

Would just laying a tape near a magnet affect the unexposed tape on the spools? Record your voice on a blank tape. Place a strong magnet and the tape together in a box. To allow enough time for any changes to occur, leave the materials in the box overnight. The next day, listen to the recording and determine the effect of the magnet on the unexposed tape.

## CHECK IT OUT!

Valdemar Poulsen (1869–1942), a Danish engineer, was the first person to use magnetized wire to make sound recordings. Since Poulsen's time, wire has been replaced with magnetic tape. Read about the history of magnetic tape recordings. Questions to think about: How did Valdemar Poulsen's wire recordings work? What materials are used now to make recording tapes? What is a stereophonic tape? How is sound recorded on the tape?

## PROBLEM

*Does hitting a magnet weaken its magnetic strength?*

## Materials

16d iron nail
bar magnet
timer
small paper clip
compass
wooden block
masking tape
hammer
adult helper

## Procedure

*WARNING: Never touch a compass with a magnet. Touching a compass with a strong magnet can change the polarity of the compass needle, causing the end marked north to become a south pole and all directions to be reversed.*

1. Magnetize the nail by laying it on the magnet for 1 minute.
2. Test the magnetic properties of the nail by touching it to the paper clip. The nail has been magnetized if the clip clings to it.
3. Lay the compass *next to* the wooden block.
4. Lay the magnetized nail *on* the wooden block so that the tip of the nail faces east. Doing this prevents the nail from being magnetized by the earth's magnetic field, which lies in a north-to-south direction.
5. Tape the nail to the block.
6. Ask an adult to strike the nail 20 times with a hammer.
7. Test the magnetic properties of the nail again by touching it to the paper clip.

## Results

The paper clip does not cling to the nail after the nail has been struck by the hammer.

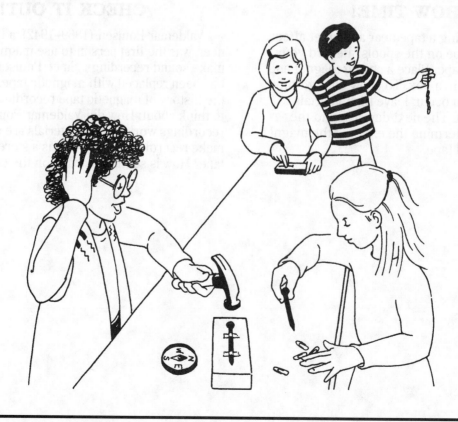

## Why?

Atoms within a magnet do not act individually, but combine to form microscopic clusters called **domains**. Atoms within the domain act like tiny magnets and line up with their north poles pointing toward the earth's magnetic north pole. When many domains of a material line up so that the north poles point in the same direction, the material becomes magnetic. Hitting the magnetized nail causes the orderly arrangement of the domains to be jarred out of place. The north poles randomly point in different directions. The nail loses its magnetic properties, and is said to be **demagnetized**.

## LET'S EXPLORE

1. Does the nail have to be struck 20 times to demagnetize it? Repeat the experiment, letting the tip of the nail extend past the edge of the wooden block so that it can be touched to a paper clip after each strike with the hammer. Record the least number of strikes required to demagnetize the nail. **Science Fair Hint:** Make diagrams showing the position of domains before and after hitting the nail and use them as part of a project display.

2. Would laying the nail in a north-to-south direction affect its ease of being demagnetized? Repeat the original experiment, placing the nail in a north-to-south direction. Again, let the tip of the nail extend past the edge of the wooden block, and touch it to a paper clip after each hammer strike. Compare the number of strikes to the number needed to demagnetize the nail in an east-to-west direction.

## SHOW TIME!

Can a nail be demagnetized by rubbing it back and forth with a magnet? Magnetize a nail and test its magnetism by touching it to a paper clip. Rub a magnet in one direction across the surface of the nail five or six times, and test the nail's magnetic properties again. Then, rub the nail in the opposite direction, and again tests its magnetic properties. Display a diagram showing the procedure of this experiment and indicate the results. Remember that demagnetized materials have domains pointing in random directions.

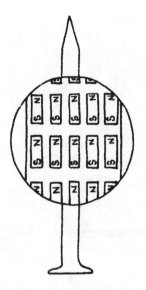

MAGNETIZED

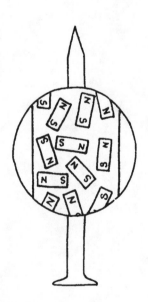

DEMAGNETIZED

## CHECK IT OUT!

Find out more about ways to reduce or destroy the magnetic properties of a magnet. Would cutting a magnet in half destroy it? How does heat affect magnetic properties? Do magnets lose their strength over time?

# Mathematics

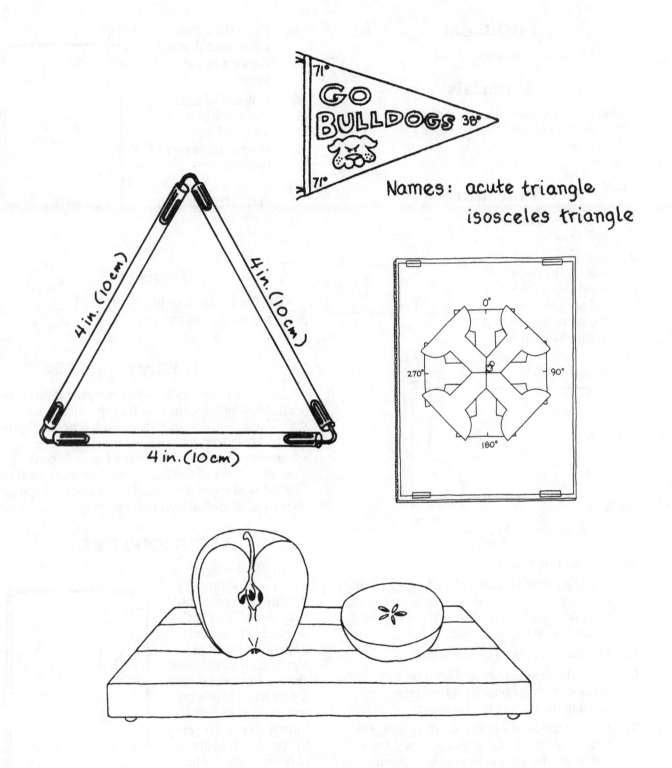

71°

GO
BULLDOGS

38°

71°

Names: acute triangle
      isosceles triangle

4 in. (10cm)

4 in. (10cm)

4 in. (10cm)

0°

270°    90°

180°

# Just Alike

## PROBLEM

*What is radial symmetry?*

## Materials

sheet of dark-colored construction paper
3-by-5-inch (7.5-by-12.5-cm) index card
pencil
scissors

## Procedure

1. Fold the paper in half twice.

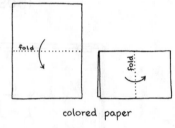

colored paper

2. Along the short end on the right-hand side of the index card, draw the pattern shown in the diagram.

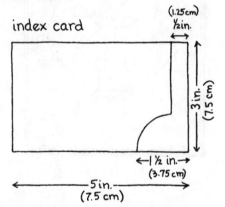

3. Cut out the pattern.

4. Lay the pattern on the colored paper so that the longest edge of the pattern is on one of the folds and the shortest edge of the pattern is on the other fold.

5. Outline the pattern on the paper.

6. Turn the design over and lay it on the **adjacent** (neighboring) folded edge. Outline the pattern on the paper.

7. Cut out the figure drawn on the paper, cutting through all four layers of paper. Do not cut along the lines in the corner, as indicated by the solid lines in the diagram.

8. Keep the cutout figure and discard the rest of the paper.

9. Unfold the figure and draw two diagonal lines across the center of the figure.

10. Study the figure and determine how many identical parts it has.

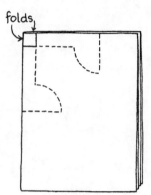

## Results

The figure has four identical parts spreading out from its center.

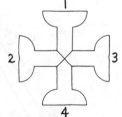

## Why?

The four parts of the figure have balanced proportions, which means that they are all the same size, shape, and distance from each other. A figure that has balanced proportions is said to have **symmetry.** Each part **radiates** (spreads out) from the center of the figure in a repeating pattern like the spokes on a wheel. This is a type of symmetry called **radial symmetry.**

## LET'S EXPLORE

Would the figure have radial symmetry if 2 different patterns were used? Repeat the original experiment, using 2 different patterns, such as the ones shown. Remember, if a figure has a repeating pattern that radiates from the center, even if the pattern repeats only once, the figure has radial symmetry.

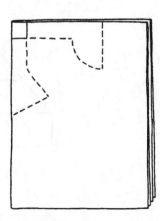

## SHOW TIME!

1. Figures have **bilateral symmetry** if, when the figure is folded on a line, the two halves are identical. The line between the two halves is called a **line of symmetry**. How many lines of symmetry are in the figure you made in the original experiment? **Science Fair Hint:** Make a diagram showing each line of symmetry in the figure. Number each of the lines. *NOTE: The figure has four lines of symmetry.*

2. Figures with radial symmetry also have rotational symmetry. **Rotational symmetry** means that one of the repeating patterns will fit into another when the figure is rotated a certain number of degrees. Demonstrate rotational symmetry by using the figure from the original experiment. Place the figure in the center of a sheet of typing paper so that the figure's straight outer edges are parallel to the edges of the paper. Draw an outline of the figure on the paper. Lay the drawing on a piece of thick cardboard about the same size as the paper, and secure the paper to the cardboard with tape. Label the four straight outer lines of the drawing 0°, 90°, 180°, and 270° as shown. Place the figure on top of the drawing, and stick a pushpin through the center of the figure, the drawing, and the cardboard. Make a mark on one of the figure's repeating patterns, then rotate the figure and find all the possible degrees at which the figure and the drawing overlap. Display this model of rotational symmetry and use it in an oral explanation of this symmetry.

3. Nature provides many examples of bilateral and radial symmetry. The flowers of orchids, snapdragons, and sweet peas have bilateral symmetry. Flowers such as roses, wild geraniums, and morning glories have radial symmetry. Study the symmetry of these and other flowers. Use photographs of flowers to prepare posters representing both types of symmetry.

4a. An apple can be used to represent bilateral symmetry. Ask an adult to cut an apple in half from top to bottom. Make a print of one half of the apple halves. Cover a paper plate with tempera paint. Rub the cut side of the apple half in the paint and then press it on a sheet of white paper. Allow the paint to dry. Look for a line of symmetry on the print. Test what appears to be a line of symmetry by folding the print in half along the line.

b. An apple can also be used to represent radial symmetry. Ask your adult helper to cut another apple across the middle. Make a print with one of the halves as before. Label the type of symmetry represented and display the print with the other one.

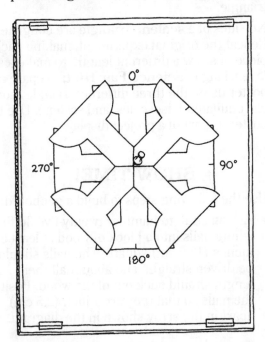

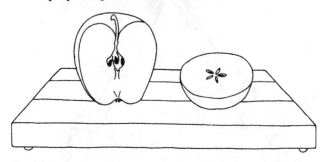

## CHECK IT OUT!

*Point symmetry* is a special type of rotational symmetry. Use a geometry text to find out more about point symmetry. Does a figure with point symmetry have bilateral symmetry? Show examples of this type of symmetry.

# Three Sided

## PROBLEM

*What is a triangle?*

## Materials

scissors
ruler
3 plastic drinking straws
3 small paper clips

## Procedure

1. Cut a 4-inch (10-cm) piece from each straw.
2. Open each paper clip as shown in the diagram.

3. Insert one bent end of each paper clip into the end of each straw piece. Adjust the angle of the bent paper clip if needed.

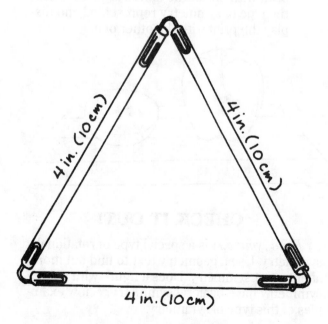

## Results

You have made a figure with three straight sides joined only where the sides meet.

## Why?

The figure is an example of a polygon. A **polygon** is a **closed figure** (a geometric figure that begins and ends at the same point) formed by three or more line segments that are joined only where the ends of the line segments meet. Each of these endpoints is connected to only two line segments. A polygon made of three sides is called a **triangle**. The sum of the angles created by the three sides is always 180 degrees. Triangles can be identified according to how many, if any, of their sides are **congruent** (the same). The triangle made in this experiment has three congruent sides and is called an **equilateral triangle**.

## LET'S EXPLORE

1. A triangle with two congruent sides is called an **isosceles triangle**. Repeat the experiment, making two pieces of straw longer or shorter than the third piece, to make an isosceles triangle.
2. No sides of a **scalene triangle** are congruent. Repeat the original experiment, making each piece of straw a different length, to make a scalene triangle. **Science Fair Hint:** Prepare a poster using the three different triangle models: equilateral, isosceles, and scalene. Use the poster as part of a project display.

## SHOW TIME!

1. Use the following steps to build a geoboard:
   - Ask an adult to hammer twenty-five 3d finishing nails into a block of wood at least 5 inches (12.5 cm) square. The nails should be driven straight, and about half their length should stick out of the wood. Position the nails so that they are 1 inch (2.5 cm) apart in the array shown in the diagram.

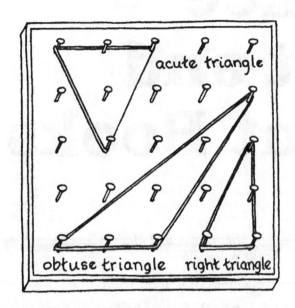

- Stretch rubber bands around the nails to create the following triangles which are identified depending on the measure of their angles:

  **acute triangle** All angles measure less than 90°.

  **right triangle** One angle measures exactly 90°.

  **obtuse triangle** One angle measures greater than 90°.

- Label each triangle and display the geoboard.

2. The area of the triangles on the geoboard can be calculated by using "Pick's formula," which is written:

$$A = \tfrac{1}{2} \times b + i - 1$$

This is read: Area ($A$) equals one-half times $b$ (the number of nails on the perimeter, or outer boundary, of the triangle) plus $i$ (the number of nails inside the triangle) minus 1. For example, for the obtuse triangle in the diagram, you would find the area by the following steps:

- Pick's formula: $A = \tfrac{1}{2} \times b + i - 1$
  $b = 4$
  $i = 2$
  $A = \tfrac{1}{2} \times 4 + 2 - 1$

- The steps in solving this problem are:

  Multiply the first two numbers: $\tfrac{1}{2} \times 4 = 2$

  Add 2 to the product: $2 + 2 = 4$

  Subtract 1 from the sum: $4 - 1 = 3$

*The area of the obtuse triangle is equal to 3 squares on the geoboard.*

3. Display items or drawing of items with triangular shapes, such as a pennant or sail on a boat. Use a **protractor** (an instrument used to measure angles in degrees) to measure the angles of each triangle. Triangles are named in two different ways: (1) according to how many, if any, of their sides are congruent, and (2) according to the measure of their angles. List both names for each triangular item displayed. Items can be displayed as shown.

For information about using a protractor, see pages 12–13 in *Janice VanCleave's Geometry for Every Kid* (New York: Wiley, 1994).

# Science Project and Experiment Books

## ASTRONOMY

VanCleave, Janice. *Astronomy for Every Kid.* New York: Wiley, 1991.

Wood, Robert W. *Science for Kids: 39 Easy Astronomy Experiments.* Blue Ridge Summit, PA: TAB Books, 1991.

## BIOLOGY

Bonnet, Robert L., and G. Daniel Keen. *Botany: 49 Science Fair Projects.* Blue Ridge Summit, PA: TAB Books, 1989.

———. *Botany: 49 More Science Fair Projects.* Blue Ridge Summit, PA: TAB Books, 1989.

Cain, Nancy Woodard. *Animal Behavior Science Projects.* New York: Wiley, 1995.

Dashefsky, H. Steven. *Zoology: 49 Science Fair Projects.* Blue Ridge Summit, PA: TAB Books, 1995.

Hershey, David R. *Plant Biology Science Projects.* New York: Wiley, 1995.

Kneidel, Sally. *Pet Bugs.* New York: Wiley, 1994.

VanCleave, Janice. *A+ Biology.* New York: Wiley, 1993.

———. *Animals.* New York: Wiley, 1993.

———. *Biology for Every Kid.* New York: Wiley, 1990.

———. *The Human Body for Every Kid.* New York: Wiley, 1995.

———. *Microscopes and Magnifying Lenses.* New York: Wiley, 1993.

———. *Plants.* New York: Wiley, 1997.

Wood, Robert W. *Science for Kids: 39 Easy Animal Biology Experiments.* Blue Ridge Summit, PA: TAB Books, 1991.

———. *Science for Kids: 39 Easy Plant Biology Experiments.* Blue Ridge Summit, PA: TAB Books, 1991.

## CHEMISTRY

VanCleave, Janice. *A+ Chemistry.* New York: Wiley, 1993.

———. *Chemistry for Every Kid.* New York: Wiley, 1989.

———. *Molecules.* New York: Wiley, 1993.

## EARTH SCIENCE

Levine, Shar, and Allison Grafton. *Projects for a Healthy Planet.* New York: Wiley, 1992.

VanCleave, Janice. *Dinosaurs for Every Kid.* New York: Wiley, 1994.

———. *Earthquakes.* New York: Wiley, 1993.

———. *Earth Science for Every Kid.* New York: Wiley, 1991.

———. *Ecology for Every Kid.* New York: Wiley, 1995.

———. *Geography for Every Kid.* New York: Wiley, 1993.

———. *Oceanography for Every Kid.* New York: Wiley, 1995.

———. *Rocks and Minerals.* New York: Wiley, 1996.

———. *Volcanoes.* New York: Wiley, 1994.

———. *Weather.* New York: Wiley, 1995.

Wood, Robert W. *Science for Kids: 39 Easy Geology Experiments.* Blue Ridge Summit, PA: TAB Books, 1991.

———. *Science for Kids: 39 Easy Meteorology Experiments.* Blue Ridge Summit, PA: TAB Books, 1991.

## MATH

VanCleave, Janice. *Math for Every Kid.* New York: Wiley, 1991.

———. *Geometry for Every Kid.* New York: Wiley, 1994.

## PHYSICS

Cobb, Vicki. *Science Experiments You Can Eat.* New York: Harper Trophy, 1994.

VanCleave, Janice. *Electricity.* New York: Wiley, 1994.

———. *Gravity.* New York: Wiley, 1993.

———. *Machines.* New York: Wiley, 1993.

———. *Magnets.* New York: Wiley, 1993.

———. *Physics for Every Kid.* New York: Wiley, 1991.

Weise, Jim. *Roller Coaster Science.* New York: Wiley, 1994.

## GENERAL PROJECT AND EXPERIMENT BOOKS

Amato, Carol J. *Super Science Fair Projects.* Chicago: Contemporary Books, 1994.

Bochinski, Julianne Blair. *The Complete Book of Science Fair Projects,* revised edition. New York: Wiley, 1996.

Bombaugh, Ruth. *Science Fair Success.* Hillside, NJ: Enslow, 1990.

Cobb, Vicki. *Science Experiments You Can Eat.* New York: Harper Trophy, 1994.

Frekko, Janet, and Phyllis Katz. *Great Science Fair Projects.* New York: Watts, 1992.

Levine, Shar, and Leslie Johnstone. *Everyday Science.* New York: Wiley, 1995.

———. *Silly Science.* New York: Wiley, 1995.

Potter, Jean. *Science in Seconds for Kids.* New York: Wiley, 1995.

VanCleave, Janice. *202 Oozing, Bubbling, Dripping, and Bouncing Experiments.* New York: Wiley, 1996

———. *201 Awesome, Magical, Bizarre, and Incredible Experiments.* New York: Wiley, 1994.

———. *200 Gooey, Slippery, Slimy, Weird, and Fun Experiments.* New York: Wiley, 1993.

Wood, Robert W. *When? Experiments for the Young Scientist.* Blue Ridge Summit, PA: TAB Books, 1995.

# Reference Books

## ASTRONOMY

Beasane, Pam. *1000 Facts about Space.* New York: Kingfisher, 1992.

Harrington, Philip, and Edward Pascuzzi. *Astronomy for All Ages.* Old Saybrook, CT: Globe Pequot Press, 1994.

Moche, Dinah L. *Astronomy: A Self-Teaching Guide.* New York: Wiley, 1989.

Pearce, Q. L. *Stargazer's.* New York: Doherty, 1991.

## BIOLOGY

Garber, Steven D. *Biology: A Self-Teaching Guide.* New York: Wiley, 1989.

Stein, Sara. *The Body Book.* New York: Workman, 1992.

## CHEMISTRY

Tocci, Salvatore. *Chemistry Around You.* New York: Prentice Hall, 1985.

## EARTH SCIENCE

Dennis, Jerry. *It's Raining Frogs and Fishes.* New York: Harper Perennial, 1992.

Forrester, Frank H. *1001 Questions Answered about the Weather.* New York: Dover, 1981.

Groves, Don. *The Oceans.* New York: Wiley, 1989.

Lockhart, Gary. *The Weather Companion.* New York: Wiley, 1988.

Tufty, Barbara. *1001 Questions Answered about Hurricanes, Tornadoes, and Other Natural Air Disasters.* New York: Dover, 1989.

## ENGINEERING

Editors of Consumer Guide. *The Big Book of How Things Work.* Lincoln Wood, IL: Publications International, 1991.

Parker, Steve. *How Things Work.* New York: Random House, 1991.

Schwartz, Max. *Machines, Buildings, Weaponry of Biblical Times.* Old Tappan, NJ: Revell, 1990.

Williams, Brian. *Science and Technology.* New York: Kingfisher, 1993.

## GENERAL SCIENCE

Bosak, Susan V. *Science Is.* New York: Scholastic, 1991.

Feldman, David. *How Does Aspirin Find a Headache?* New York: Harper Perennial, 1994.

Holzinger, Philip R. *The House of Science.* New York: Wiley, 1990.

Kerrod, Robin. *Book of Science.* New York: Simon and Schuster, 1991.

Roberts, Royston M., and Jeanie Roberts. *Lucky Science.* New York: Wiley, 1995.

## MATH

Kenda, Margaret, and Phyllis S. Williams. *Math Wizardry for Kids.* Hauppauge, NY: Barron's, 1995.

Salem, Lionel, Frederic Testard, and Coralie Salem. *The Most Beautiful Mathematical Formulas.* New York: Wiley, 1992.

## PHYSICS

Bohren, Craig F. *What Light through Yonder Window Breaks?* New York: Wiley, 1991.

Walker, Jearl. *The Flying Circus of Physics with Answers.* New York: Wiley, 1977.

# Sources of Scientific Supplies

## CATALOG SUPPLIERS

Carolina Biological Supply Company
2700 York Road
Burlington, NC 27215
(800) 334–5551

Connecticut Valley Biological Company
82 Valley Road
P.O. Box 326
Southampton, MA 01073
(800) 628–7748

Cuisenaire
10 Bank Street
P.O. Box 5026
White Plains, NY 10606
(800) 237–3142

Delta Education, Inc.
P.O. Box 915
Hudson, NH 03051-0915
(800) 258-1302

Fisher Scientific
Educational Materials Division
485 South Frontage Road
Burr Ridge, IL 60521
(708) 655–4410
(800) 766–7000

Frey Scientific Division of Beckley Cardy
100 Paragon Parkway
Mansfield, OH  44903
(800) 225-3739

NASCO
901 Janesville Avenue
P.O. Box 901
Fort Atkinson, WI 53538
(800) 677–2960

Sargent-Welch
911 Commerce Court
Buffalo Grove, IL 60089
(800) 727–4368

Ward's Natural Science
5100 West Henrietta Road
Rochester, NY 14586
(800) 962–2660

## SOURCES OF ROCKS AND MINERALS

The following stores carry rocks and minerals and are located in many areas. To find the stores near you, call the home offices listed below.

Nature Company
750 Hearst Avenue
Berkeley, CA 94701
(800) 227-1114

Nature of Things
10700 West Venture Drive
Franklin, WI 53132–2804
(800) 283–2921

The Discovery Store
15046 Beltway Drive
Dallas, TX 75244
(214) 490–8299

World of Science
900 Jefferson Road
Building 4
Rochester, NY 14623
(716) 475–0100

# Glossary

**abiotic** Nonliving.

**acute triangle** A triangle in which all angles measure less than 90°.

**analyze** To examine carefully and in detail.

**anatomy** The study of the structure of plants and animals.

**arteries** Blood vessels that carry blood away from the heart.

**asthenosphere** The portion of the mantle below the lithosphere.

**astronomy** The study of stars, planets, and other objects in the universe.

**atom** The building unit of matter.

**atrium** The upper chamber of a heart.

**attraction** The force that draws things together.

**auxin** A plant chemical that causes plant cells to grow longer.

**bar graph** A diagram that uses bars to represent data.

**batholith** A large intrusion below the earth's surface.

**behaviorism** The study of actions that alter the relationship between an organism, such as a plant or an animal, and its environment.

**bilateral symmetry** Symmetry in which the two halves of a figure are identical when divided by a line of symmetry.

**biology** The study of living things.

**biotic** Living.

**botany** The study of plants and plant life, including their structure and growth.

**buoyancy** The upward force exerted by a fluid, such as water or air, on an object in the fluid.

**cast** A solid reproduction of an organism, having the same outer shape as the organism, which is made by filling a mold with a substance such as mud or plaster that hardens.

**cell** The smallest unit, or building block, of an organism.

**chart** Data or other information in the form of a table, graph, or list.

**chemical particles** Atoms and molecules.

**chemistry** The study of the materials that substances are made of and how they change and combine.

**choroid** A thin layer of heavily pigmented tissue in the eye that absorbs light rays.

**chromosomes** Threadlike structures in a cell that carry instructions, much like a computer program, to make the cell function.

**cleavage** The tendency of a mineral to break along a smooth surface.

**closed figure** A geometric figure that begins and ends at the same point.

**cohesion** The attraction between like chemical particles.

**coleoptile** The protective covering over the undeveloped shoot of a monocot embryo.

**compound machine** A machine made of two or more simple machines, such as levers.

**compress** To press materials together.

**condensation** The process by which a vapor changes into a liquid due to a removal of heat energy.

**congruent** The same.

**contract** To draw together.

**control** A test in which all variables are identical to the experiment being performed except the independent variable.

**controlled variable** Something that is kept the same in an experiment.

**core** The innermost and hottest section of the earth.

**corona** The layer of glowing gas around the sun.

**cotyledon** The seed leaf that stores food for a plant embryo until it can make its own food.

**crust** The thin outer covering of the earth.

**crystal** A solid made up of atoms arranged in an orderly, regular pattern.

**culms** Upright grass stems above ground.

**cuticle** Dead skin around the base and sides of the fingernail.

**data** In this book, data is observations and/or measured facts obtained experimentally.

**demagnetize** To reduce or eliminate magnetic properties by causing the domains to be less uniform.

**density** The "heaviness" of an object, based on its mass compared to its volume.

**dependent variable** The variable being observed in an experiment which changes in response to the independent variable.

**dew** Water droplets formed when water vapor in the air comes in contact with cool surfaces and condenses.

**dew point** The temperature at which dew forms.

**dicotyledon** or **dicot** A plant that has two cotyledons.

**dike** A narrow, vertical intrusion that rises and breaks through horizontal rock layers.

**direct current** (DC) An electric current that flows only in one direction.

**domain** A microscopic cluster of atoms whose north poles point in the same direction.

**dominant gene** A gene that, when present, determines the trait of an offspring.

**earthquake** A violent shaking of the earth's crust caused by a sudden movement of rock beneath its surface.

**earth science** The study of the earth.

**ecological community** The interaction of living organisms with their environment.

**ecologist** A scientist who studies organisms and their environment.

**ecology** The study of the relationships of living things to other living things and to their environment.

**ecosystem** A distinct area that combines biotic communities and the abiotic environments with which they interact.

**ectothermic** ("outside heat") Cold-blooded; having a body temperature that changes with the environment.

**effort arm** The distance from the effort force to the fulcrum of a lever.

**effort force** A force that is applied.

**electric conductor** A material through which electrons move easily.

**electric current** A flow of electrons.

**electricity** The form of energy associated with the presence and movement of electric charges.

**electromagnet** A coil of wire that has become magnetized by passing a flow of electric current through it.

**electrons** Negatively charged particles of an atom.

**embryo** An organism in its earliest stage of development.

**embryonic** Undeveloped.

**energy** The capacity to do work.

**engineering** The application of scientific knowledge for practical purposes.

**epicenter** The point on the earth's surface directly above the focus of an earthquake.

**epicotyl** The part of the plant embryo, located above the hypocotyl, that develops into the plant's stem, leaves, flowers, and fruit.

**equilateral triangle** A triangle with three congruent sides.

**erosion** The wearing away of the earth's surface, usually by wind or water.

**evaporate** To change from a liquid to a gas due to an addition of heat energy.

**experimentation** The process of testing a hypothesis.

**exploratory experiments** As defined in this book, experiments in which the data is part of the research.

**fertilization** The joining of an ovum and a sperm to form a zygote.

**fixed pulley** A pulley that stays in place as it turns.

**focus** The point at which earthquake vibrations begin.

**fossil mold** An impression of an organism within a rock cavity.

**fossils** Remnants or traces of prehistoric life-forms preserved in the earth's crust.

**freezing nuclei** Surfaces, such as dust particles or raised edges on rough surfaces, on which ice crystals can form.

**freezing point** The temperature at which a liquid changes to a solid.

**fulcrum** The fixed point of rotation on a lever.

**fungus** (plural **fungi**) A simple, plantlike organism that cannot make its own food.

**gear** A wheel with teeth around its outer rim.

**gene** Locations on a chromosome that determine inherited traits.

**genetics** The study of the methods of transmission of qualities from parents to their offspring; the principles of heredity in living things.

**geology** The study of the composition of the earth's layers and its history. See also the subtopics **mineralogy, seismology, volcanology, fossils,** and **rocks.**

**geometry** The branch of mathematics that deals with points, lines, planes, and their relationships to each other.

**germination** The process by which a seed begins to grow.

**gravity** The force that pulls celestial bodies, such as planets and moons, toward each other; the force that pulls things on or near a celestial body toward its center.

**guanine** A chemical in the back of the eye of night hunters, such as cats, that reflects light, thus causing the eye to appear to glow.

**heat** The total energy of all particles in an object.

**heredity** The passing on of traits from parents to offspring.

**hilum** The light-colored, oval-shaped scar on a seed coat.

**homogeneous** The same throughout.

**humidity** The amount of water vapor in the air.

**hybrid trait** A trait that results from a combination of nonidentical gene pairs.

**hygrometer** An instrument used to measure humidity.

**hypha** (plural **hyphae**) Any of the threadlike parts that make up the mycelium of a fungus.

**hypocotyl** The part of the plant embryo that develops into the roots and, very often, the lower stem of the plant.

**hypothesis** An idea about the solution to a problem, based on knowledge and research.

**icicle** A mass of hanging ice that is formed by the freezing of dripping water.

**igneous rock** Rock formed by the cooling and solidification of magma.

**imprint** Marks made by pressing; impressions made by organisms in soft mud that were preserved when the mud solidified.

**independent variable** A manipulated variable in an experiment that causes a change in the dependent variable.

**inertia** Resistance to a change in motion.

**inhibit** To keep from happening.

**inorganic** Not formed from plants or animals.

**insulator** A material that slows down the transfer of heat energy.

**internode** The area on a plant stem between two consecutive nodes.

**intrusion** A flow of magma that cools and hardens before it reaches the surface.

**intrusive volcanism** The movement of magma within the earth.

**isosceles triangle** A triangle with two congruent sides.

**journal** A written record of your project from start to finish.

**kinetic energy** Energy of motion.

**laccolith** A domed-shaped intrusion that has pushed up the overlying rock layers.

**lava** Magma that has reached the earth's surface.

**lever** A simple machine, consisting of a rigid bar and a fulcrum, that is used to lift or move things.

**ligament** A tough band of tissue connecting the ends of bones.

**line graph** A diagram that uses lines to express patterns of change.

**line of symmetry** A line that divides a figure into two identical halves when the figure is folded along the line.

**lithosphere** The uppermost layer of the earth which includes all of the crust and the uppermost part of the mantle.

**load** The object being lifted or moved by a machine such as a lever.

**lunula** The whitish, half-moon-shaped area of the fingernail, beneath which all growth of the nail takes place.

**luster** Shininess.

**machines** Devices that make work easier.

**magma** Molten rock beneath the surface of the earth.

**magnetic field** The invisible pattern of magnetism around a magnet.

**magnetism** The force of attraction or repulsion between magnetic poles, and the attraction that magnets have for magnetic materials.

**magnitude** A measurement of the amount of shaking energy released by an earthquake.

**mammal** Any warm-blooded, hairy animal that has a backbone.

**mantle** The middle section of the earth, between the core and the crust.

**mass** The amount of material in an object.

**mathematics** The use of numbers and symbols to study amounts and forms. See also **geometry.**

**mechanical advantage** (MA) The amount by which a machine increases an effort force.

**mechanical energy** The energy of moving objects; potential energy and kinetic energy.

**melanin** A pigment that determines color of hair, skin, and other animal tissues.

**metamorphic rock** Rock formed from other types of rock by pressure and heat.

**metamorphism** The process by which rock changes from one form to another due to pressure and heat.

**meteorology** The study of weather, climate, and the earth's atmosphere.

**microbiology**   The study of microscopic organisms, such as fungi, bacteria, and protista.

**microgravity**   A minute amount of gravitational pull as measured in space.

**micropyle**   The small dot at one end of a hilum.

**midocean ridges**   Cracks in the crust of the earth that extend into the mantle, caused by the upward flow of magma.

**mineral**   A solid formed in the earth by nature from substances that were never a plant or animal.

**mineralogy**   The study of the composition and formation of minerals.

**mold**   A growth, usually fuzzy, produced on food and damp surfaces; a cavity in which an object can be shaped.

**molecule**   The smallest particle of a substance that retains the properties of the substance.

**monocotyledon** or **monocot**   A plant that has one cotyledon.

**motor effect**   Movement that results from placing a wire carrying a direct current in a magnetic field.

**mycelium**   The tangled mass of hyphae in a fungus.

**nail bed**   The pink, fleshy area beneath the fingernail that provides a smooth surface for the nail to grow across.

**nail root**   The area beneath the lunula of a fingernail where nail growth occurs.

**negative phototropism**   Plant growth away from light.

**nitrogen-fixing bacteria**   Bacteria that change nitrogen gas into usable nitrogen compounds for plant use.

**node**   The joint on a plant stem where a leaf is generally attached.

**obtuse triangle**   A triangle in which one angle measures greater than 90°.

**oceanography**   The study of the oceans and marine organisms.

**orbit**   The curved path that a satellite traces around a celestial body.

**orbital period**   The time required to complete one orbit.

**organic**   Formed from living matter.

**organisms**   Living things.

**ovum** (plural **ova**)   A female sex cell, or egg.

**paleontology**   The study of prehistoric life-forms.

**pantograph**   A compound machine used to change the size of a drawing.

**penicillium**   A bluish green mold used to make the antibiotic penicillin and cheeses such as Roquefort.

**penumbra**   The lighter outer part of a shadow.

**phloem tubes**   Plant tubes that transport sap containing food manufactured in the plant's leaves throughout the plant.

**photosphere**   The visible surface of the sun.

**phototropism**   The growth response of plants to light.

**physical science**   The study of matter and energy.

**physics**   The study of forms of energy and the laws of motion. See also **electricity, energy, gravity, machines,** and **magnetism.**

**physiology**   The study of life processes, such as respiration, circulation, the nervous system, metabolism, and reproduction.

**pictograph**   A chart that contains symbols representing data.

**pie chart**   A circle graph that shows information in percentages.

**pigment**   Coloring matter.

**pithy**   Soft and spongy.

**plasticity**   The ability of a solid material to flow.

**plumule**   The part of a plant embryo, located at the tip of the embryonic shoot, that consists of several tiny, immature leaves that at maturity form the first true leaves.

**polygon**   A closed figure formed by three or more line segments that are joined where the ends of the line segments meet.

**positive phototropism**   Plant growth toward light.

**potential energy**   Stored energy.

**pressure**   A force applied over an area.

**primary research**   Information collected on one's own.

**problem**   A scientific question to be solved.

**project conclusion**   A summary of the results of project experimentation and a statement that addresses how the results relate to the hypothesis.

**project experiment**   An experiment designed to test a hypothesis.

**project research**   Research to help you understand the project topic, express a problem, propose a hypothesis, and design one or more project experiments.

**project report**   The written record of your entire project from start to finish.

**protractor**   An instrument used to measure angles in degrees.

**pulley**   A machine that consists of a grooved wheel, called a pulley, that holds a cord and is used especially to lift weights.

**Punnett square** A method of showing all the possible gene combinations that are transferred from parents to offspring.

**pupil** The dark opening in the eye.

**pure trait** A trait that results from the combination of identical gene pairs.

**purpose** The scientific problem that has been identified by research and about which a hypothesis is made.

**radial symmetry** Symmetry in which all parts of a figure radiate from the center in a repeating pattern like spokes on a wheel.

**radiate** To spread out.

**radicle** The tip of the hypocotyl which develops into the roots of a plant.

**ratio** A numerical comparison between two different things.

**recessive gene** A gene that does not determine the trait of an offspring when a dominant gene is present.

**reflex action** An automatic, involuntary action that does not require thinking.

**repulsion** The force that keeps things from drawing together.

**research** The process of collecting information and data about a topic being studied.

**resistance arm** The distance from the load to the fulcrum of a lever.

**resistance force** The weight of a load lifted or moved by a machine.

**revolve** To move in an orbit around an object.

**rift valley** A crack in an underwater mountain chain that extends into the earth's mantle.

**right triangle** A triangle in which one angle measures exactly 90°.

**rock** A solid made up of one or more minerals.

**rock cycle** The never-ending process by which rocks change from one type to another.

**rotate** To turn on an axis.

**rotational symmetry** Symmetry in which one repeating pattern of a figure fits into another when the figure is rotated a certain number of degrees.

**salinity** The measure of the amount of salt dissolved in water.

**saltern** A place where salt is produced by the solar process.

**sap** A watery liquid containing minerals and food that moves through a plant's vascular system.

**satellite** A celestial body that revolves about another celestial body.

**saturated air** Air that is full of water vapor.

**saturated solution** A solution in which a solvent contains the maximum amount of dissolved solute.

**scalene triangle** A triangle with no congruent sides.

**science project** An investigation using the scientific method to discover the answer to a scientific problem.

**scientific method** The process of thinking through the possibilities of solutions to a problem and testing each possibility for the best solution.

**secondary research** Information and/or data that someone else has collected.

**sedimentary rock** Rock formed by deposits of sediment, or small particles of material deposited by wind, water, or ice.

**seed** The part of a plant that contains the plant embryo and a stored food supply for the embryo, and that is protected by a seed coat.

**seed coat** The outer protective covering of a seed.

**seedling** A young plant grown from seed.

**seismic P-wave** The primary pressure wave of an earthquake.

**seismogram** A written record of the amount of shaking energy released by an earthquake.

**seismograph** An instrument used to measure and record the shaking energy of an earthquake.

**seismology** The study of earthquakes.

**senses** Sight, hearing, taste, touch, and smell.

**sensory** Having to do with the senses.

**shoot** The part of a plant that grows above ground.

**sill** A thin, horizontal intrusion that is sandwiched between other rock layers.

**solar eclipse** The blocking of the sun's light by the moon when the moon passes directly between the sun and the earth.

**solar process** The production of salt by the evaporation of seawater.

**solar salt** Salt produced by the solar process.

**solute** A substance that breaks into smaller parts and moves throughout a solvent; the substance in lesser quantity in a homogeneous solution.

**solution** The homogeneous mixture of a solute with a solvent.

**solvent** A substance in which a solute dissolves; the substance in greater quantity in a homogeneous solution.

**specific heat** The amount of heat needed to raise the temperature of 1 pound of a substance 1 degree Fahrenheit (1 g of a substance 1°C).

**sperm**   A male sex cell.

**spinal cord**   A cord running through the center of the disks of a backbone.

**spontaneous generation theory**   The theory that living organisms come from nonliving material.

**spore**   A one-celled body produced by certain organisms, such as fungi, which can develop into a new organism.

**stimulus** (plural **stimuli**)   Anything that causes a response in an organism.

**stock**   An intrusion that is smaller than a batholith.

**streak**   The color of the powder left when a mineral is rubbed against a rough surface that is harder than the mineral.

**subcooled water**   Liquid water below the freezing point.

**symbiosis**   A relationship in which two organisms living together are mutually benefited.

**symmetry**   The property of having balanced proportions—parts that are the same size, shape, and distance from each other.

**table**   A diagram that uses words and numbers in columns and rows to represent data.

**third-class lever**   A lever in which the effort force is between the fulcrum and the load.

**tissue**   A group of cells that perform a special function.

**topic research**   Research used to select a project topic.

**traits**   Characteristics that help to identify a living organism, such as hair color, eye color, and height.

**transform**   To change from one form to another.

**transpiration**   The process by which plants lose water vapor through their leaves.

**triangle**   A three-sided polygon.

**turgidity**   Firmness due to turgor pressure.

**turgor pressure**   Internal pressure in a cell due to movement of water into the cell.

**umbra**   The darker inner part of a shadow.

**valve**   A structure that controls blood flow in one direction.

**variable**   Something that has an effect on an experiment. See also **independent variable, dependent variable,** and **controlled variable.**

**vascular plant**   A plant that has a vascular system.

**vascular system**   A plant system containing bundles of vascular tubes.

**vascular tubes**   Tubes that transport sap in plants; xylem tubes and phloem tubes.

**veins**   In a leaf, conducting structures made of bundles of vascular tubes that form the framework through which sap flows; in animals, blood vessels that carry blood to the heart.

**ventricle**   The lower chamber of a heart.

**vibrate**   To shake back and forth repeatedly.

**viscometer**   A meter used to measure the flow rate of a fluid.

**viscosity**   A liquid's resistance to flow.

**volcanology**   The study of volcanoes.

**volume**   The amount of space an object occupies based on its length, width, and depth.

**water vapor**   Water in the gas state.

**weathering**   The breakdown of rock into smaller pieces by natural processes.

**weight**   The force with which an object is pulled toward the center of the earth due to gravity and mass.

**wilt**   To become limp.

**work**   Results of a force moving an object.

**xylem tubes**   Plant tubes that transport sap containing water and minerals upward from the roots through the plant.

**zoology**   The study of animals, including their structure and growth.

**zygote**   A fertilized ovum.

# Index